D0020822

4

UNCERTAIN HAZARDS

UNCERTAIN HAZARDS

Environmental Activists and Scientific Proof

Sylvia Noble Tesh

Cornell University Press Ithaca and London

Copyright © 2000 by Cornell University

All rights reserved. Except for brief quotations in a review, this book, or parts thereof, must not be reproduced in any form without permission in writing from the publisher. For information, address Cornell University Press, Sage House, 512 East State Street, Ithaca, New York 14850.

First published 2000 by Cornell University Press

Printed in the United States of America

Library of Congress Cataloging-in-Publication Data

Tesh, Sylvia Noble, 1937–
    Uncertain hazards : environmental activists and scientific proof / Sylvia Noble Tesh.
        p. cm.
    Includes bibliographical references and index.
    ISBN 0-8014-3533-1 (cloth)
    1. Environmentalism—Social aspects.   I. Title.
GE195 .T43 2000
363.7—dc21   00-021269

Cornell University Press strives to use environmentally responsible suppliers and materials to the fullest extent possible in the publishing of its books. Such materials include vegetable-based, low-VOC inks and acid-free papers that are recycled, totally chlorine-free, or partly composed of nonwood fibers. Books that bear the logo of the FSC (Forest Stewardship Council) use paper taken from forests that have been inspected and certified as meeting the highest standards for environmental and social responsibility. For further information, visit our website at www.cornellpress.cornell.edu.

Cloth printing   10 9 8 7 6 5 4 3 2 1

FSC FSC Trademark © 1996 Forest Stewardship Council A.C.
SW-COC-098

For my daughters, Diana and Carolyn,

and for Carol

Contents

Acknowledgments

The best part about preparing to write this book was interviewing environmentalists. As I look back now it seems that everyone I talked with was friendly, eager to share experiences, and more than generous with his or her time. Many grassroots activists invited me to their homes, supplied me with tea or coffee, showed me the extensive files that documented their battle, and talked and talked. Activists working on regional and national issues were no less helpful. We usually met in their offices, and most half-hour appointments ended up stretching to a least twice that time. Unfortunately, however, only a few of these men and women actually make an appearance in this book. My theme shifted as the book took shape, and I am saving much of the information they gave me for another project. But I thank all of them here. I would not have dared to write about the environmental movement without them. They brought to life the academic books and articles I was reading.

In Connecticut I learned much from Bob Hemstock, Robert Howard, Lynne Ide, Suzanne Mattei, Janice Nuzzo, Marie Ostrander and Marie Tuccitto. In Colorado I was helped by conversations with Walter Jessel, Elizabeth Otto, Rocky Smith, and Ann Vickery. In Oregon both Bonny Hill and Carol Van Strum taught me a lot. In Michigan the incomparable Grace Lee Boggs gave me some of her precious time. So did David Berry, Hank Dertian, MaryBeth Doyal, Tracy Easthope, Pam Frucci, Ed McArdle, Kathy Milberg, Judy Roberts, Donele Wilkins, and Guy Williams. In Massachusetts I got splendid help from Abagail Avery and Gary Cohen and in Pennsylvania from Randall Brubaker and Greg Schirm. In Wyoming I was enormously fortunate to be able to interview

Mardie Murie. In New York I had valuable telephone conversations with Jan Alexander, Joann Hale, Louella Kenny, and Barbara Quimby.

In Washington, D.C., the following people taught me far more than I could have learned from books: John Adams, Jackie Warren, and Deborah Sheiman at the Natural Resources Defense Council; Michael McClosky, Blake Early, George Coling, and Joel Feigenbaum at the Sierra Club; Michael Clark at the Environmental Policy Institute; Jerry Poje at the National Wildlife Federation; Hank Cole and David Zwick at Clean Water Action; Kenny Bruno and Jerry Leape at Greenpeace; Fred Krupp at the Environmental Defense Fund: Jim Maddy at the League of Conservation Voters; and Lois Gibbs, Steve Lester, and Mike Williams at the Center for Health, Environment and Justice (which actually is just outside of Washington).

I also owe many thanks to the environmental scientists who read portions of this book and advised me on revisions: Dick Clapp, Sam Epstein, Howard Frumkin, Tom Robbins, and Steve Wing. In addition I am grateful for the help from other environmental scientists who were willing to be interviewed as the book was taking shape: Karim Ahmed, Sandra Avol Geschwind, Bill Hirzy, Rufus Morison and Frederica Perrera.

Four wonderful student research assistants kept me afloat, as well as in good spirits, as they cheerfully and competently searched the University of Michigan libraries and the Internet: Marnie Boardman, Cindy Colen, Julia Henn, and Torri Estrada. In addition, I was much helped early in the project by Yale University, which awarded me a John F. Enders Research Assistance grant, and later by the University of Michigan, which gave me a grant from the Office of the Vice President for Research.

I thank *Policy Sciences* for permission to print a modified version of Chapter Five, which originally appeared as "Citizen Experts in Environmental Risk" *Policy Sciences* 32(1):39–58, March 1999. I thank *Polity* for permission to print in Chapter Six sections of "Identity Politics, Disinterested Politics and Environmental Justice" which appeared in *Polity* 18(3):285–305, Spring 1996.

I am especially indebted to my faculty colleagues. Bruce Williams was my coauthor for the first version of Chapter Six. Crisca Bierwert, John Bound, Helen Fox, Arline Geronimus, Margaret Keck, David Meyer, Michael Ross, David Schlosberg, Nathan Teske, and Susan Wright helped along the way with critiques of the growing manuscript. Gregory Button, Mary Summers, Sarah Ritchie, and Carolyn Wang supplied me with useful information at critical periods. And Carol Rose was always ready to lend her discerning eye, her keen intellect, and her inexhaustible good humor.

UNCERTAIN HAZARDS

Overview

This is a book about the effects of social movements on societies. The theme is unusual in current studies of social movements; scholars more commonly consider the effects of societies on the formation and success of movements. But social movements can profoundly influence what people believe to be right and wrong, true and false. Such beliefs distinguish one culture from another and one historical period from another. I use the environmental movement to illustrate these effects of social movements, taking environmentalists as the creators and the promoters of a set of principles that have changed our understanding of nature and have laid the foundation for social change.

Thinking of social movements in this way addresses an intellectual dilemma: What should we do when democracy and science clash? This dilemma may not seem at first glance to involve a social movement, yet it is constantly faced by people who join grassroots groups protesting exposure to environmental pollution and by scholars studying this kind of activism. On the one hand, you have communities exercising democracy. Groups of aggrieved citizens, the victims of self-interested and powerful social actors, petition the government for redress on the basis that pollution endangers their health. On the other hand, you have scientists searching for truth. Reputable researchers, trying to learn whether exposure to the pollution in question is a public health hazard, find either no evidence or only uncertain evidence that it is. This dilemma suggests that the public and scholars must choose between two troublesome positions. They can side with democracy and support the citizens' group, even if the group has scientifically indefensible notions about disease causality, or they can side with science and support the researchers, even if doing so means discounting the claims of people with serious health problems living in the midst of toxic substances.

Fortunately there is a third position, the one I take in this book. This position puts science and democracy in the same camp. It treats science as a social construct, seeing scientific processes and pronouncements as reflections of the culture in which scientists live. Although much of the scholarly work on the social construction of science concentrates on negative aspects of cultures that have produced racist and sexist science, I write here about a new, generally positive aspect of culture—the development of environmentalism. I suggest that at least some portion of the debate among scientists about the health effects of exposure to pollution is an artifact of the relative newness of environmentalist ideas in modern societies. As these ideas become taken for granted, science will change, and is changing, to reflect them.

I came to this position on environmentalism after dozens of informal, open-ended interviews with environmental activists, most of them members of organized environmental groups. Although these groups constitute only one portion of the environmental movement—many influential environmentalists are not aligned with any movement organization—they are a critical component, because to most members of the general public they represent environmentalism. I talked with activists in three kinds of organizations: mainstream groups, grassroots groups, and grassroots support groups. These categories are not hard and fast, but they are useful for distinguishing among three different kinds of missions.

The mainstream groups focus primarily on federal laws and regulations. Most of their projects concern the protection of natural resources. They have offices in Washington, D.C., well-paid staffs, and a variety of good contacts in Congress and the Environmental Protection Agency. The two oldest mainstream groups are the Sierra Club (established in 1892) and the National Audubon Society (established in 1905); both were originally part of the conservation movement but now are devoted to broader environmentalist concerns.[1] Today, ten or so other mainstream groups exist. The major ones are the Environmental Defense Fund, the Natural Resources Defense Council, the National Wildlife Federation, the World Wildlife Fund, the Nature Conservancy, the Wilderness Society, and the Izaak Walton League.

The grassroots groups are usually little interested in protecting natural resources. Most of them form to protect people from a polluted environment. Typically, they work to prevent a proposed hazardous waste incinerator or landfill from being sited in their neighborhood or to get redress for a newly discovered problem such as contaminated water. For the most part, the members of these groups have not been politically active before, and the groups usually disband when they reach their goals or when members get too tired to fight any more. Their "offices" are in a member's basement or dining room; their "staffs" consist of the most committed members. Their budgets are minuscule; they learn as they go along. They first appeared in this country in the 1970s, gaining national attention when the Love Canal Homeowners Association was formed in 1978, and their number has been growing ever since. No one knows how many such groups exist at any given time, but there are probably many thousands. They have names such as FACE (For a Clean Environment), SAFE (Southington Association for the Environment), and PEG (Pollution Exterminators Group).

The organizations I call the grassroots support groups are the newest phenomenon. As the name implies, they exist to help local organizations. Although none has a big budget, they all have real offices and paid staffs. They provide information on mobilizing members, running meetings, using scientific data, talking with the media, pressuring policy makers, and dealing with stress. They also run periodic conferences to bring local activists together. The largest and best-known support group is the Center for Health, Environment, and Justice, located just outside of Washington in Falls Church, Virginia. The fact that CHEJ was originally called the Citizens Clearinghouse for Hazardous Waste illustrates the broadening agenda of these support groups. Similar organizations around the country, but with a more regional focus, include the Ann Arbor Ecology Center, the Southwest Network for Economic and Environmental Justice, the Colorado Environmental Coalition, the Delaware Valley Toxics Coalition, and the Northwest Coalition Against Pesticides. In addition, both the Sierra Club and Greenpeace—mainstream organizations in that they have offices in Washington, work on national legislation, and were originally established to protect nature—offer support to grassroots groups.

These three kinds of environmental groups draw on great quantities of widely available information that indicates that the environment we live in is heavily polluted with industrial chemicals. Consider these quotations:

"Nearly 70,000 chemical products have been introduced since World War II and 1,500 new ones are added each year. Total U.S. production of chemicals amounts to over 300 million tons annually."[2]

"[I]n 1994, 22,744 facilities released 2.26 billion pounds of listed toxic chemicals into the environment."[3]

"[I]n 1994 approximately 62 million people... lived in counties where air quality levels exceeded the national air quality standards for at least one of the six principle pollutants."[4]

"The EPA's Toxic Release Inventory... states that manufacturing industries discharge 180 thousand tons of toxins into surface water, with the chemical, paper, and metals industries contributing the largest shares. Yet this estimate excludes major nonmanufacturing sources such as utilities, mining, and military production and is totally inconsistent with the amount reported in the government's database of permitted discharges. In the latter database, plants reported discharging a thousand times more toxins than in the TRI estimate, and for just six of the hundreds of chemicals listed in the TRI."[5]

"Last year, 46 contaminants, from dioxin to chlordane, were found in fish. The number of lakes, rivers, and other U.S. waterways where consumers have been advised to avoid or limit consumption of trout, salmon, or other species because of chemical contamination rose from 1,278 in 1993 to 1,740 in 1995."[6]

"In 1995 over forty million Americans were served by drinking water systems with lead levels exceeding the regulatory action level."[7]

"By September 1995, a total of 1,374 sites had been listed or proposed for listing [on the Superfund's National Priority List].... In addition, EPA had identified 40,094 potentially hazardous waste sites across the nation. About 94 percent of these sites have been assessed by EPA to determine if further action is needed. By the end of 1995, EPA had removed 24,472 low-priority sites, leaving 15,622 remaining in the inventory."[8]

"In 1993 over 40 percent of the Hispanic population, and over 35 percent of the Asian/Pacific population was exposed to poor air quality."[9]

"Three out of every five Black and Hispanic Americans live in communities with uncontrolled toxic waste sites."[10]

I cite these data partly because I have chosen to begin the book with a chapter that raises doubts about the necessity for environmental activism. Lest some readers should decide I am an industry apologist and toss the book aside after the first chapter, I want to make it clear that there are plenty of reasons to worry about environmental pollution in this country.

Chapter One tells three stories about communities that mobilized to protest exposure to environmental pollutants. In Guilford, Connecticut, residents living on one block where five people had brain cancer, sued the local electric company for exposing them to electromagnetic fields. Around Alsea, Oregon, a group of women with a high rate of miscarriages pressured the Forest Service to stop spraying their farms and roads with an herbicide containing dioxin. At Love Canal, New York, people with a variety of health problems fought to be evacuated from their homes, which were located alongside a leaking hazardous waste landfill. All of these organized citizens can claim at least some kind of victory. The extent to which policy analysts and the general public should praise these grassroots activists, however, is not clear, for in all three cases the science supporting the activists' claims is either missing or uncertain.

Chapter Two explains why it is hard for scientists to find data supporting the claims of grassroots groups. The chapter focuses on risk assessment, the process adopted by the EPA to determine whether exposure to industrial pollution could be responsible for a community's health problems. The central problem with risk assessment is that the knowledge needed to link pollution with disease is usually hidden from scientists. The bulk of the research on the health effects of pollution is done on laboratory animals. But test animals are necessarily exposed to much higher doses of suspect chemicals than are human populations, and species vary greatly in their response to chemicals, so extrapolating to human beings is guesswork. Studies of human populations, however, also fail to provide clear information. The populations exposed are usually too small, information about exposure levels is usually too weak, the latency period before cancer shows up is usually too long, and the possible confounding factors are usually too many. Thus, scientists can seldom find more than a weak link between a community's health problems and environmental pollution.

Chapter Three, asking what might prompt scientists to do different kinds of research, describes the principles at the heart of the environmental movement. It identifies three core environmentalist principles: one scientific, one ethical, and one political. The scientific principle says that all of nature is interrelated like a web and that human interference is likely to be harmful. The ethical principle says that nature has its own integrity and should not be used by human beings for their own purposes. The political principle says that nature is seriously endangered and needs our protection. These principles, new in industrial society since the 1960s, represent a sharp break from the past, when most people assumed that nature existed to serve human beings and could recuperate from whatever uses people made of it. Despite their newness, the principles have been widely embraced by Americans. Polling and survey data suggest that, for many people, these three principles have now become simple common sense.

Chapter Four begins by recounting the social constructivist argument that science cannot be entirely objective because it is inescapably influenced by culture. Just as racism and sexism have subtly influenced investigators, so have pre-environmentalist assumptions about nature. The constructivist argument implies that, as environmentalist principles become taken for granted in contemporary culture, science will change. In fact, there are several signs that such a change is occurring. One sign is the development of a broader focus in risk-assessment research, going beyond cancer to include reproductive and other outcomes of exposure. Another sign is the identification of two especially sensitive populations, children and racial minorities. A third is the use of biomarker research to expand the definition of disease beyond clinical illness. A fourth is the argument that validity standards should be lowered so that more research findings will be deemed statistically significant. Thus, the situation depicted in Chapters One and Two—the lack of scientific corroboration of grassroots activists' claims—may be an artifact of the slow incorporation of environmentalism into science rather than a statement about the actual effect of pollution on health.

Chapter Five is a critique of the literature on risk perception, which shows that laypeople perceive risk differently from experts. It is also a critique of the literature on risk communication, which counsels government agencies to respect laypeople's perceptions. The chapter argues that although individual laypeople may indeed construe risk differently from experts, government agencies deal with organized groups, not with individuals, and organized groups consult, employ, and have access to many experts. This chapter describes the expertise used by the Natural Resources Defense Council in the Alar case in 1989, and it reports on the expertise available to grassroots groups as well. The chapter concludes that debates over the health effects of environmental pollution are conflicts among experts, not conflicts between citizens and experts.

Chapter Six illustrates the widespread acceptance of environmentalist ideas among the general public. It introduces the concept of experiential knowledge and, drawing on statements by people who have actually experienced life in heavily polluted neighborhoods, demonstrates that grassroots activists quickly see causal relationships between exposure to pollution and disease. The chapter then describes variations on the theory that the life experiences of socially marginal people provide them with more-accurate views of the world than do the experiences of more-favored groups. But, it argues, raw experience cannot explain people's knowledge. In the case of exposure to environmental pollution, marginalized people's knowledge about its effect on health comes from their (often unconscious) adoption of environmentalist views about the consequences of mistreating nature.

Chapter Seven opens with a discussion of social movement theory, noting the emphasis most scholars place on explaining how social movement organizations form and what makes them successful. It argues that the focus on organizations limits our ability to understand how social movements affect culture. Social movement theory does provide some extremely useful concepts. Among them is the idea that movements reframe familiar events and situations, turning them into injustices. But the chapter argues that social movement frames are not just lying around to be picked up and used. They have to be created and then continually reinforced and enhanced. A view of social movements focusing on this frame-developing task makes room for a whole array of movement actors, usually left out of social movement studies.

1 Protest against Pollution

Since the 1960s—and from some perspectives a great deal longer—citizens in communities all over the United States have organized to remedy, stop, or prevent environmental pollution.[1] Sometimes the pollution has been in the air, the soil, or the water for a long time but has just now been recognized. Sometimes the pollution is something that is expected to accompany a proposed hazardous waste facility or a new industrial plant. In either case, citizens fear for their health. Angry at both business and government, they write letters, visit legislators, consult experts, call town meetings, testify at public hearings, file lawsuits, and march on government buildings and business headquarters. A theme running through all these activities is that citizens should, and can, participate in the decisions that affect their lives. It's a principle at the core of democracy.

The principle is supported by democracy theorists and social movement scholars writing about the outcome of citizen participation. Some scholars find participation desirable because it alerts governments to new public problems.[2] Others praise participation for making people into more informed, and thus better, citizens.[3] A third group applauds it for building community and engendering new, positive identities.[4] Yet others say it can check the power of elites and provide an alternative to despair and defeat.[5]

The three stories I tell in this chapter illustrate all these praiseworthy effects. Each presents an ordinary citizen who made a difference. The stories also raise a disturbing question. What if the citizens were wrong? What if the pollution in their communities was not a health hazard after all? The scholars I just cited envision citizens as participating in issues based on moral or political claims. In such cases, no one has the authority to say the claims are erroneous. But although citizens who organize against environmental pollution do use moral concepts, their claims have a scientific base. They say that environmental pollution causes disease. If scientists call that claim inaccurate, the participation itself looks questionable. Consider what happened in Guilford, Connecticut, in Alsea, Oregon, and at Love Canal, New York.

Guilford, Connecticut

The ordinary citizen in Guilford was Bob Hemstock, a self-employed salesman and inventor. In 1990 Hemstock began a long struggle to warn people about the dangers of exposure to EMFs—the low-level electromagnetic fields generated by power transmission lines.

Hemstock's campaign started in mid-January of that year, after he had learned from friends one evening that on Meadow Street, where the friends (and Hemstock's grown son) lived, five people had brain cancer. Meadow Street, which is just one block long, only has nine houses, so the ratio of cancers to houses seemed to Hemstock wildly out of line. His friends said that the neighbors had treated the situation simply as a misfortune; it was sad, but it was the kind of thing that happens sometimes. Hemstock, however, believed there was an environmental explanation for the cancers, and he plunged immediately into a crusade on behalf of the neighborhood. At first he did not think of what later seemed the obvious villain: the enormous, humming electricity substation that takes up a good portion of the west side of Meadow Street. As he told me in an interview later that year:

> I first thought of chemicals or some kind of pollution because of Love Canal. I got samples of tap water and had it tested at UConn. But it tested OK. So then I checked the medical supply factory over by the salt marsh.... They wouldn't give me a list of their chemicals, but I called back and said I had an idea for a first-aid kit that they might produce and I needed to know what chemicals they used. So this sales rep got interested and gave me the whole list. I took the list to the Guilford public library and looked up every chemical. But none of them were listed as carcinogens.
>
> Then I thought of PCBs [polychlorinated biphenyls] and the substation. PCBs are carcinogens, and they're used to insulate electric wires.... So I called the electric company and I got this lady on the phone and I asked her if they knew about all the brain cancers on

Meadow Street and if the substation could be the cause. But she right away got mad and told me that there was a lot of crazy stuff published about electromagnetic fields but none of it was true. That's when I realized that EMFs might be the problem.... I went back to the libraries—to the Guilford library and to the medical library at Yale—and I discovered 130 medical studies showing that EMFs cause brain cancer.[6]

Furious at the disjuncture between what he had read and the apparent absence of protective public policies, Hemstock called a meeting of Meadow Street residents. He told them about his research and advised them to sue Northeast Utilities. He thought the company should either shut down the substation or buy the residents' houses. Hemstock also telephoned the Guilford Health Department, a local television station, and Paul Brodeur—a staff writer for the *New Yorker* whose name he had run across in the library—to spread the word about the brain cancers and the power station on Meadow Street.

His actions stirred up a lot of activity. Some of the Meadow Street residents took his advice and filed a lawsuit against Northeast Utilities. The Guilford Health Department instituted a telephone survey of the neighborhood. The television station broadcast interviews with four residents who described their poor health, and several local newspapers, as well as the *New York Times,* printed similar stories. The Connecticut Department of Health Services, which had been notified by the Guilford Health Department, turned its attention to electromagnetic fields for the first time and did an epidemiological investigation of the Meadow Street situation.

In addition, as I learned later from a health department epidemiologist, Hemstock's actions eventually led the Connecticut legislature to establish an interagency task force charged with developing a policy on EMF exposure. Among its activities, the task force held a three-day public conference in the summer of 1992 to get citizen input on the policy. A hundred and fifty people attended, including a panel of national experts in pertinent fields. Subsequently, a group of citizens in Fairfield, about 35 miles west of Guilford, formed an organization to protest the siting of power lines near the public schools.[7]

Hemstock's contact with Paul Brodeur may have had the most widespread impact. In a long, angry *New Yorker* article about Meadow Street, Brodeur referred to many studies in the scientific literature on EMFs.[8] the *New Yorker* piece added weight to Brodeur's earlier book on electromagnetic fields[9] and prompted the U.S. Department of Labor to request the White House Office of Science and Technology Policy (OSTP) to undertake an EMF study.[10] The article, of course, also spread the word to the *New Yorker's* readers, thus affecting (to some unknown degree) Americans' worry that electromagnetic fields around high-power lines pose a serious, hidden health hazard.[11]

Brodeur's readers had reason to be worried. By 1990 at least four peer-reviewed epidemiological studies had demonstrated a positive relationship between cancer and exposure to the low-level electromagnetic field around power lines. The first one found that children living in houses near high-power lines in Denver were two to three times more likely to die of cancer (primarily leukemia and nervous system tumors) than were other children.[12] Later, the same investigators found similar results for adults in Denver and in Longmont, Colorado, where exposed people had high rates of cancers of the nervous system, breast, and uterus.[13] Other investigators found a high rate of childhood cancer near high-power lines in Rhode Island.[14] A fourth study, done in Sweden also found that, compared with controls, children in homes near power lines were more likely to have leukemia and nervous system tumors.[15]

In addition to this research on people living in houses near power lines, by 1990 at least nine studies had correlated disease with occupational exposure to EMFs. The most consistent finding was that electrical workers have a significantly elevated risk of leukemia. Other data also linked electrical occupations to brain tumors.[16]

Hemstock's contribution to publicizing these findings did not stop with his initial calls to the residents, health department, and media. He put in hours of work on the Guilford case. As he told me, "I double checked everything for Paul [Brodeur]. I did the legwork for the article. I walked the whole distribution line five times." All this work was fueled by an abiding commitment to democracy.

> I would do anything to get publicity on this to the average person.... Everyone assumes that government works for you, but it doesn't. I put government and business in the same perspective. Government will say whatever it needs not to lose votes. Business will say whatever it needs not to lose bucks. I know that sounds communistic, but I don't mean it that way. I'm patriotic. When they play the national anthem at ball games I put my hand over my heart. But I've changed as I've gotten older. I see that things don't work. We still have the best country, but we need to make it better. We need to get people involved.... Voting has gone down every year because people say you can't fight city hall. But you can.[17]

Exposure to low-level radiation from electromagnetic fields, however, may not actually be a public health hazard. Electrical workers do seem to be at risk; the scientific evidence is fairly clear about that. But, as many experts are quick to point out, negative studies on the general population outweigh positive ones. Articles in the peer-reviewed literature routinely note the absence of scientific consensus on the effects of exposure to EMFs.[18] T. S. Tenforde says that "it is extremely difficult to interpret the results of recent epidemiological studies that have reported a correlation between cancer incidence and exposure to... magnetic fields."[19] M. Granger Morgan says that "the relationship between exposure and risk may involve something other than the product of field strength and time."[20] Reviewing the literature on EMFs and childhood cancers, Jack Siemiatycki says that "the scientific question of whether there are such health effects is far from resolved."[21] And Bengt Knave concludes that, "International guidelines state that the scientific knowledge on magnetic fields and cancer does not warrant limiting exposure levels for the general public."[22] Most recently, researchers at the National Cancer Institute completed a large study that found no link between magnetic fields and leukemia in children,[23] and the National Research Council announced that electromagnetic fields do not pose a health hazard.[24]

Critics of the thesis that magnetic fields are dangerous can also point to the two investigations specifically prompted by the Meadow Street case. The White House Office of Science and Technology Policy said that "there is no convincing evidence in the published literature to support the contention that exposures to extremely low-frequency electric and magnetic fields (ELF-EMF) generated by... local power lines are demonstrable health hazards."[25] And the Connecticut Department of Health Services said much the same thing about Guilford. After the department had concluded its epidemiological study on Meadow Street, it called a public meeting in the Guilford library and announced that there was no true cluster of brain cancers on Meadow Street and there was no excess number of brain cancers in Guilford as a whole.[26]

Bob Hemstock left that meeting in a muted fury. ("During the meeting I was fuming, but under the advice of the lawyers I didn't say anything."[27]) He embarked on a long project to collect information on EMFs and cancer. By 1992 he had data on all six of the shoreline towns east of New Haven. "I can't believe what a massive cover-up this is, from the government right down to the newspapers.... No one realizes how much EMFs affect us all. Someday they will. People will say, 'I wish I had listened.' A lot of people will have died because of the coverup."[28]

Alsea, Oregon

The ordinary citizens in Alsea, Oregon, were a young couple named Steve and Carol Van Strum who, in 1974, moved with their four children from Berkeley, California, to an old farm in the beautiful Five Rivers Valley on Oregon's central coast. One day, a year or so later, they had a frightening experience when a passing Forest Service truck accidentally sprayed a cloud of herbicides on the children as they played near the farmhouse. The children were acutely ill for a few days, and so was Carol Van Strum, who had rushed through the cloud when she heard the children's shrieks. After everyone had recovered, Carol and Steve began an investigation into herbicides. They contacted the Forest Service to find out what was in the spray, then went to the Oregon State University library to learn about its health and environmental effects. While they were gathering information, they realized that plants and animals on their farm had also been affected by the herbicide and that herbicide sprays had frequently settled around them in the past.[29]

In January 1976, the Van Strums wrote a letter to the local newspaper objecting to herbicide spraying. The herbicide, they said, routinely drifted to their farm and had caused deformities in their chicks and ducklings, damaged their vegetable crops, and made their children ill. They said they had discovered that 2,4,5-T, the principal ingredient, contains dioxin, a highly toxic substance capable of causing birth defects and cancer in extraordinarily small doses. They pointed out that 2,4,5-T (and thus dioxin) was sprayed in Vietnam during the war and was responsible for malformed babies and carcinoma of the liver in that country.

To the Van Strums' surprise, the letter elicited a huge response. People phoned and wrote them from all over the area, telling about their experiences with damages to crops, wildlife, and their own health. More important, two readers called a public meeting. The meeting, attended by old-time valley residents as well as many newcomers, had two immediate consequences. One was the founding of Citizens Against Toxic Sprays (CATS). The other was the filing of a lawsuit against the Forest Service. In a conversation with me years later, Carol Van Strum said,

There were several initial meetings. We got together once, and everyone agreed we should do something, and we really thought all we had to do is tell the Forest Service that there was a problem and they would say, "Oh, we won't do it anymore." So we met with the Forest Service. Well, they refused to even take seriously what we were saying, much less agree not to spray around us, and so we, everybody, got together again and decided maybe we should go see a lawyer.[30]

In March, CATS sued the Forest Service for filing an inadequate Environmental Impact Statement (EIS). A core group then spent the next three months preparing their case. Their lawyer, Van Strum told me, "encouraged us to do as much as we could to reduce [his fees], so we learned a lot in a very short time." She laughed in recollection.[31] By the time the case came to court, the members of CATS were able to submit "massive testimony to the judge on the toxicity and environmental fate of... 2,4,5-T, from scientists all over the United States."[32] As a result, the judge ordered a temporary injunction against spraying 2,4,5-T in any national forest until the Forest Service filed an adequate EIS statement.

The impact of CATS spread well beyond the injunction itself, however. First of all, the planning for the lawsuit brought a lot of disparate individuals together. Some eighty families lived in the valley, and nearly all of them joined CATS. Carol Van Strum said,

I thought it was really neat that scientists and loggers and housewives and schoolteachers and farmers could get together and agree on something. And millworkers, that was really wonderful. The mill had its own little town and everything, and almost all the people who worked at that mill were very, very involved in CATS.... Then people in Eugene heard about it. And for some reason it caught people's imagination over there. I don't know why. It was the counterculture. A lot of college students, that's what most of them were. They all became part of CATS. They were a tremendous help. They held benefit concerts. We never could have raised enough money without them.... And there were also the Hoedads. They were a collective labor group that did reforestation work.[33]

CATS also laid the foundation for a permanent and much larger antipesticide organization. Not long after the lawsuit was settled, CATS disbanded. The organization had existed only as a vehicle for the litigation, so its dissolution signaled victory not defeat. In its place rose another and more comprehensive organization called NCAP, Northwest Coalition Against Pesticides, with headquarters in Eugene. NCAP, which celebrated its twentieth anniversary in 1997, now has a membership of 2,000 people and a "contact database" of 15,000. It serves organic farmers, homeowners, and grassroots activists, providing information on the properties of commercial pesticides and on alternatives to pesticides. On the policy level, one goal is to require pesticide manufacturers to include inert ingredients on their products' labels; another is to require public reporting of pesticide use.

The other legacy of CATS is the EPA's ban on dioxin in herbicides. CATS got so many requests for information about herbicides that members compiled a fact sheet, and eventually they began distributing it all over the valley. During the summer of 1977 in Alsea, several miles west of Five Rivers Valley, a schoolteacher named Bonnie Hill picked up one of the fact sheets at a crafts fair and began to wonder whether the miscarriage she had had two years earlier, and the miscarriages of some of her former students, could have resulted from exposure to dioxin. So she decided to collect data. She visited every woman she could find in the valley who had had a miscarriage.

> The whole process took me a long time, because I was teaching full time and I had my family to care for. By the Spring of '78 I found eight women who had eleven miscarriages altogether. They all occurred in the springtime. I hadn't found *any* that occurred at any other time of the year.[34]

Hill then went after spray data. She called and visited the Forest Service, the Bureau of Land Management, and the timber companies, trying to find out what, when, and how much they had sprayed in the last few years.

> I got varying degrees of cooperation [but] gathered... data as best I could. I mapped where the women lived in relation to the spray sites and put it together on a chart. It certainly appeared to me that there was a correlation between the timing of the spraying and the miscarriages that occurred nearby, but only a much larger study would show if that was a consistent pattern.[35]

In April 1978, Hill wrote up her findings in a one-page letter, added a copy of the chart, and, having little idea how to get action, simply sent copies to "everyone we could imagine that might be interested."[36] Fortunately for the women, a researcher from Friends of the Earth (FOE) discovered the copy that went to the EPA in Washington, D.C. Fortunately, also, and unbeknownst to the residents of Alsea, the EPA had announced just two months earlier that it would discontinue the registration of 2,4,5-T unless the manufacturers could show that the compound was safe. So the letter landed in a fertile field. The FOE researcher threw his energy into publicizing it. He contacted the press, notified other environmentalists, lobbied legislators, and harangued his friends among the EPA staff. Unresponsive at first, the EPA administration finally sent a team to Oregon to conduct a new, and larger, inquiry into the Alsea miscarriages.

Compared with Bonnie Hill's study, the EPA's study collected spray data for many more years, and over a much wider area. Instead of relying on subjective reports of miscarriages, it got information from hospital records. And it had controls, comparing Alsea with two unsprayed areas. The results corroborated Hill's findings: compared with controls, women living around Alsea had three times the rate of spontaneous abortions in June, and those abortions were correlated with the spraying of the dioxin-contaminated herbicide.

The EPA immediately announced an emergency suspension of the use of 2,4,5-T and another compound called Silvex throughout the United States except for rangelands and ricefields. The EPA's announcement, on February 28, 1979, specifically attributed the suspension to the results of the Alsea study.[37] It provides a fitting cap to the story begun three years earlier, when the Van Strums became grassroots activists.

But can dioxin actually cause women to miscarry? Those who say no seem to have the upper hand. The EPA's Alsea study was not strong enough to have been submitted for publication and is not even referenced in the agency's comprehensive 1994 draft report on dioxin.[38] The study's weaknesses were obvious from the beginning, even to environmentalists, who attacked it for relying on inadequate exposure and medical data.[39] The nay-sayers can also argue that research outside the Alsea area is at best inconclusive. The 1994 EPA document on dioxin lists fourteen studies investigating the link between exposure to 2,4,5-T and miscarriages. Six found "weak but consistent associations"; eight found no association. The EPA concluded, "Overall, it must be acknowledged that the data compiled to date are inadequate to address this issue."[40]

Even fewer studies on dioxin and miscarriages had been done at the time the EPA suspended 2,4,5-T. When I called the EPA's regional office in Seattle to get an explanation for the suspension, the toxicologist I talked with said, "It was a politicized, goofy situation, a real emotional thing. We don't even have that study anymore. I don't think they even have it in D.C. . . . . It was probably a change for the better to restrict 2,4,5-T, but there's no real proof that it causes miscarriages. It was done more for social reasons than for science."[41]

Carol Van Strum disagrees. Since the disbanding of CATS she has remained a committed activist. She works now mainly with Physicians for Social Responsibility (PSR) and was an organizer of the 1996 PSR conference in Salem, Oregon, on dioxins and health. The previous year she contributed to a popular book on dioxin, writing that "the Alsea study confirmed the link between dioxin exposure and the appalling human effects suffered by [people] in the study."[42]

Love Canal, New York

At Love Canal, the ordinary citizen was Lois Gibbs, a twenty-seven-year-old housewife who initially was just trying to transfer her sickly son out of a contaminated elementary school. The Love Canal story, which has been told many times, begins in 1976.[43] Early that year, scientists working for the International Joint Commission (a U.S.–Canadian alliance) found in Lake Ontario fish that had been contaminated with an insecticide called Mirex. They alerted the New York Department of Environmental Conservation (DEC), which traced one source of the Mirex to an old landfill in the city of Niagara Falls.

The landfill—a sixty-foot-wide canal dug and then abandoned in the 1890s by an entrepreneur named William Love—had been a burial ground for chemical wastes between 1942 and 1953. At the time of the Mirex discovery, only a big grassy field marked the canal's location. An elementary school stood just off its center, and it was surrounded by a community of modest homes. People living there had complained off and on about chemical odors for many years, and some even knew about the buried dump, but apparently no one had considered the Love Canal to be a health hazard.

The DEC discovery that chemicals were migrating from the canal came at a time when the chemical smells began to increase. In addition, by the mid-1970s large holes occasionally opened up in the field around the school; standing puddles of chemical-laden water appeared; and buried canisters and barrels had begun to surface. A thick black substance oozed onto the walls and floors of some people's basements; sump pumps occasionally brought up thick liquid; and a backyard swimming pool was pushed up two feet out of the ground.

None of this, however, prompted the residents to organize. For nearly two years after Mirex had been traced to the landfill—until the middle of 1978—the Love Canal story is about government agencies.

Initially, the agencies did very little. During the first year, the DEC tried without success to learn from the original dumpers what chemicals had been buried in the landfill and to get the New York Department of Health to test the soil. The city of Niagara Falls did hire a private company to draw up plans for sealing the site and building a drainage system, but it decided that it could not afford to have the work done. The county health department refused to act at all, downplaying any danger and taking the position that in any case individual homeowners were responsible for protecting themselves from pollution. But in September of 1977, U.S. Congressman John LaFalce learned about the migrating chemicals and asked the regional EPA office to investigate. The regional director, on seeing the conditions at Love Canal, alerted Washington, and in October 1977 the federal EPA began collecting and analyzing air samples from the basements of Love Canal homes.

In the meantime, the New York Department of Health had finally agreed to test the soil. When the chief laboratory scientist there realized that the samples came from a residential area, he notified the New York Commissioner of Health. The commissioner flew out to Love Canal from Albany in April 1978, surveyed the situation, and announced publicly that it presented a potentially serious health hazard. He then set in motion an extensive epidemiological study of the residents' health. The study included a door-to-door survey, a long questionnaire, and the taking of blood samples.

By May 1978, the EPA had gathered enough information from its air-sampling study to repeat the state health commissioner's announcement that the pollution posed a public health hazard. On August 2, 1978, the New York State Commissioner of Health went well beyond his earlier remarks and declared a health emergency at Love Canal. He recommended that in the first ring of houses around the canal families with pregnant women or children younger than two should leave the area. He also announced that the city and county of Niagara Falls would begin a huge construction project to seal off the canal and that the state health department would join the city and county in a new health study. Five days later, Governor Hugh Carey announced that the state would purchase the 239 homes in the two rings closest to the canal to make it possible for the families to move. On the same day as Governor Carey's announcement, President Jimmy Carter declared Love Canal a disaster area.

The reasons for all this activity were the discovery that many more toxic chemicals besides Mirex had broken out of the canal and the finding that women living on the streets closest to the canal had an elevated rate of miscarriages. In the words of the Department of Health,

> [U]nacceptable levels of toxic substances associated with more than 80 compounds were emanating from the basements of many homes in the first ring directly adjacent to the Love Canal.... Eleven of these are known [to] or suspected of causing cancerous growth in laboratory animals, and one—benzene—is a well-established human carcinogen.... As can be seen from this list [of compounds and their acute and chronic effects] virtually all of man's physiologic systems can be pathologically influenced by exposure to chemicals identified to date at the Love Canal site.
>
> [T]he relative odds ratio for miscarriages among women living on the Canal was 1.49, or nearly one and one-half times the expected rate within the general population. A more detailed breakdown of [the epidemiological] data by residents of the northern and southern sections indicated that the highest frequency of miscarriages (up to 3.45 times the expected frequency for women ages 30–34) occurred among residents of the southern Canal section.[44]

At that point, from the government's perspective, the events at Love Canal had peaked: officials had discovered a potentially serious health problem, determined its extent, and initiated the measures necessary to protect the public. But Lois Gibbs saw the issue differently.

Earlier in the summer, the school principal had turned down Gibbs's request that her son transfer to another school. Convinced that her son's poor health was caused by the chemicals, Gibbs decided to try to get the school closed down. She drew up a petition and began knocking on doors asking neighbors to sign.

> As I proceeded down 99th Street, I developed a set speech. I would tell people what I wanted. But the speech wasn't all that necessary. It seemed as though every home on 99th Street had someone with an illness. One family had a young daughter with arthritis.... Another daughter had had a miscarriage. The father, still a fairly young man, had had a heart attack.... As I continued going door to door, I heard more. The more I heard, the more frightened I became. This problem involved much more than the 99th Street School. The entire community seemed to be sick![45]

During the weeks she was circulating the petition, Gibbs and other Love Canal residents were learning about the health and environmental testing from media accounts—mainly a string of articles by Michael Brown in the *Niagara Gazette*—and from a series of public meetings called by city and state agencies. In addition, Gibbs was turning for information to her brother-in-law, a biologist who was knowledgeable about chemicals and had experience in community organizing. The more she learned, the greater the discrepancy seemed between the situation and what the government was doing about it. Gradually, she changed her goal from protecting her son's health to protecting the health of *everyone* living in the area.

This was different from the government's goal. Or, to be more precise, although the government also wanted to protect everyone's health, it had its own definition of who was at risk. The difference was made clear when the state Department of Health announced at a public meeting on August 2 that pregnant women and families with children under two in the first ring of houses should leave Love Canal. Gibbs, who attended the meeting, jumped up and cried, "If the dump will hurt pregnant women and children under two, what for God's sake, is it going to do to the rest of us?" Another woman whose house backed up on the canal called out, "Wait a minute, wait a minute. My kids are *over* two. Are you trying to tell me my children are safe?"[46]

From this anger was born the Love Canal Homeowners Association, with Lois Gibbs as president. Over the next twenty-one months Gibbs and the members of the association did everything they could think of to publicize the health hazards at Love Canal. They held dozens of press conferences, gave interviews on radio and television (notably the *Phil Donahue Show* and *Good Morning America,* but also less well-known programs), toured the canal with visiting officials, picketed President Carter at the Buffalo airport, demonstrated in front of the Niagara Falls city council offices, burned effigies of the governor and health commissioner, filed an injunction against the remedial construction site on the ground that it endangered residents' health, carried mock coffins to Albany, picketed the remedial construction site for weeks and got arrested for it, visited the EPA in Washington, brought Jane Fonda to speak to residents, testified at a congressional hearing and a state senate hearing, wrote hundreds of letters to government officials at all levels, and held two EPA officials hostage for six hours.

It was after the EPA hostage episode, in May 1980, that President Carter declared a second emergency at Love Canal and offered federal funds for temporary relocation of the 550 remaining families. In June, Governor Carey requested federal funds for purchase of their homes. And on July 3, the U.S. Congress approved an emergency appropriation of $20 million, thereby allowing everyone to leave.

Five months after the appropriation, Congress passed CERCLA, the Comprehensive Environmental Response, Compensation, and Liability Act, commonly known as the Superfund. The law recognizes inactive hazardous waste sites as a critical health and environmental problem and establishes a protocol to clean them up. Most observers credit the long struggle at Love Canal for inspiring the law.[47]

Many scientists, however, question whether Love Canal was ever a serious health hazard. No one doubts that a great many toxic chemicals leaked from the landfill. At issue is their effect on public health. Skeptics can start with the 1978 health survey by the New York Department of Health, which found a high rate of miscarriages and justified moving pregnant women and children out of the area. This conclusion, which was never published except in a Department of Health pamphlet meant for the governor and state legislators, was apparently premature. Clark Heath, from the Centers for Disease Control and Prevention, says that the study found "no clear increased risk" of miscarriages or birth defects among women living in Love Canal. It did find an increase in low-birth-weight babies, but the increase was not correlated with actual exposure to the canal.[48] Skeptics can also note that even the politically progressive authors of the National Research Council's 1991 book on environmental epidemiology omitted miscarriages and birth defects from their discussion of the peer-reviewed literature on Love Canal.[49]

Skeptics can go on to the six other Love Canal investigations—one on cancer rates, two on low-birth-weight babies, one on childhood illness, and two on chromosomal damage. These investigations also raise questions about the claim that Love Canal was a health crisis. The study on cancer rates examined data for all cancers between 1966 and 1977 and went back to 1955 for data on liver cancer, leukemia, and lymphoma. It showed no excess cancers attributable to the chemicals among people at Love Canal.[50] The two studies on birth weight are contradictory. One found an increase in the percentage of low-birth-weight babies born between 1940 and 1953, just before and during the years when the dump was in active use, but no such increase between 1953 and 1978.[51] The other study did find a later increase, one in the percentage of low-birth-weight babies born between 1965 and 1978.[52] The childhood illness study showed that, compared with controls, Love Canal children had an elevated prevalence of seven health problems: skin rashes, eye irritation, seizures, hyperactivity, abdominal pain, incontinence, and learning problems. But the authors themselves noted that the last four could have been due to stress and that all the information may have been biased because it came from mothers' reports, not physicians'.[53]

The study most vulnerable to criticism is one of the two on chromosome damage. It was commissioned by the EPA and was considered important because exposure to chemicals can affect chromosomes, and chromosome damage may predict future risk of cancer and genetic disorders. Although the study did find eight people with abnormalities among the thirty-six residents studied,[54] the EPA called the investigation useless, largely because it lacked contemporary controls.[55] A second study, using blood samples from forty-six residents and from a group of controls, found that Love Canal residents had no more chromosome damage than did people who lived nearby but had not been exposed to the leaking chemicals.[56]

The scarcity of positive studies has not deterred the former residents of Love Canal. In 1996, I talked on the phone with four of the six women who had been the core activists in the Love Canal Homeowners Association. Every one of them spoke with a mixture of residual anger at what they had to go through and pride at its outcome. "I'm proud we were able to succeed," said one woman. "We proved you can fight city hall. And not just city hall, but New York State, and the federal government. A small group can get something accomplished."[57] As for Lois Gibbs, she moved from Love Canal to the Washington, D.C., area in 1980 and the next year founded CCHW, the Citizens Clearinghouse for Hazardous Waste. Renamed the Center for Health, Environment and Justice in 1997, the organization now helps over 8,000 grassroots groups fight against environmental pollution.[58]

How should one respond to these three stories? Certainly they are not anomalous. In many communities, citizens valiantly struggle against exposure to environmental pollution, but critics argue that only weak or contested evidence supports them. Among these communities are Tacoma, Washington;[59] Times Beach, Missouri;[60] Woburn, Massachusetts;[61] Yucca Mountain, Nevada;[62] Three Mile Island, Pennsylvania;[63] and Santa Clara, California.[64] Grassroots activists have an almost routine response to the critics: They say that studies that do not confirm the dangers of environmental pollution are done by industry pawns.[65] Social scientists and other professionals, for their part, take several positions. Some pay scant attention to the scientific controversy and report instead on the considerable psychological stress of living amid hazardous waste.[66] Others focus on the controversy and conclude either that grass-roots activists perceive risk in a peculiar way,[67] or that they are uneducated and hysterical.[68] In the next chapter I take none of those paths. Instead, I ask why scientific studies so infrequently support grassroots groups' reports that their health is endangered.

2 · Environmental Health Research

In the mid-1980s most government agencies concerned with health or the environment adopted a formal process for determining whether a particular source of pollution could be responsible for a community's health problems.[1] The process, initially set out in 1983 by the National Research Council, is called risk assessment and has been widely hailed for establishing a common nomenclature among scientists and regulators, standardizing the methodology for studying environmental pollutants, and giving government agencies a firm scientific foundation on which to set environmental health policies.[2]

Certainly it is easy to see risk assessment as a step forward, especially if, as William Ruckelshaus says, "The establishment of formal public rules... reduces the possibility that an EPA administrator may manipulate the findings of some [study] so as to avoid making the difficult, and perhaps politically unpopular choices involved in risk management decisions."[3] But the adoption of risk assessment represents a radical shift in emphasis at the EPA. When the agency was founded in 1970, its primary question was the same as the environmentalists' question: How can we protect the environment from pollution? The emphasis reflected the federal environmental policy stated in the National Environmental Policy Act of 1969: "To declare a national policy... to promote efforts which will prevent or eliminate damage to the environment and biosphere."[4] Now the EPA is asking, "Exactly how hazardous is pollution?"[5]

There are no simple answers to either question, but the first one assumes the existence of harmful pollution and directs public attention to the political and engineering strategies for combat. It calls on creative and multiple strategies, promising a continual struggle until pollution is conquered, or at least significantly reduced. The second question *contests* the existence of harmful pollution and directs attention to the scientific methodologies for identifying cause and effect. It calls on proper procedures and closely followed rules of evidence, promising the discovery of new knowledge about environmental pollutants.

What interests me here is the fact that the new knowledge so infrequently shows that exposure to pollution causes health problems. Why should this be? The link between environmental pollution and a community's diseases seems so obvious to people in the community and to community activists and their supporters. Why can't scientists find it? That question, it turns out, plagues environmental scientists as well as onlookers like me. A major theme running through their published research is that most of the information they need to know is simply unavailable. Thus they have to use proxy information. They make laboratory data stand in for human experience, short time periods represent long ones, small communities symbolize large ones, and proximity to hazardous substances substitute for actual exposures. As a result, and for reasons I will explain in this chapter, their findings are likely to be either negative or only weakly supportive of grassroots groups' assertion that pollution is a public health hazard.

Risk Assessment Defined

Risk assessment, applicable either to proposed industrial projects or to current situations, is based on the following scenario:

> A substance leaves a source (e.g., an industrial facility), moves through an environmental medium (e.g., the air), and results in an exposure (people breathe the air containing the chemical). The exposure creates a dose in the exposed people (the amount of the chemical entering the body, which may be expressed in any of several ways), and the magnitude, duration, and timing of the dose determine the extent to which the toxic properties of the chemical are realized in exposed people (the risk).[6]

In its influential 1983 report (Nicholas Ashford called the report "near-legendary"[7]), the National Research Council divided this scenario into four steps. In the first step, called hazard identification, scientists determine whether the chemical or mix of chemicals in question is dangerous, how much of it is in the environment, and under what conditions people living nearby could be exposed to it. In the second step, called dose-response assessment, they consider how much exposure to the hazardous material would have to occur before people would become sick. In the third step, called exposure assessment, they identify the population that might be exposed to the substances, the route through which exposure could occur, and the length of time people could be exposed. In the final step, called risk characterization, they combine the information from the first three steps and produce a number indicating the likelihood that the substances will harm people.[8]

Although community groups worry about a whole range of health problems that could be caused by pollution, most risk assessments are about cancer. Comparatively few assessments investigate other possible outcomes of environmental exposure, such as reproductive problems, nervous system or immune system effects, breathing disorders, or liver and kidney problems. The focus on cancer has two pragmatic explanations: the Environmental Protection Agency decided early on to use cancer to represent all environmentally linked diseases in risk assessment because it believed that cancer is the most sensitive indicator of risk, and standardization of data had been developed only for cancer.[9] But highlighting cancer makes the first two steps in risk assessment, hazard identification and dose-response assessment, problematic because there is no straightforward way to know whether a substance causes cancer in human beings short of deliberately experimenting on them. With today's laws and ethical principles prohibiting such investigations, the simplest and cheapest way to find out if an environmental pollutant is a carcinogen is to turn the problem over to the biochemists.

Short-Term Tests

Since the early 1970s biochemists have been investigating carcinogenicity with a variety of relatively quick in vitro tests based on the assumption that carcinogens are also mutagens. In these tests, a suspect chemical is added to a petri dish of bacteria, and if the bacteria mutate, the chemical is deemed a possible carcinogen and subject to new testing. Researchers have discovered some important carcinogens in this way, including the flame retardant Tris and tar-based hair dyes. Such discoveries provide risk assessors with information for the hazard identification step in risk assessment and give citizens, scientists, and regulators reason to worry about environmental pollutants. The problem with short-term tests, however, is that they are not very dependable. They identify several classes of known carcinogens as safe, and they identify various noncarcinogens—vitamin C, for example—as causing cancer.[10] In one evaluation of the tests, they failed to recognize 40 percent of seventy-three known carcinogens.[11] With a high rate of false positives and false negatives, short-term tests have limited application. Certainly they are not a reliable means, all on their own, to find out if a pollutant causes cancer. I describe them here because the risk assessment guidelines allow federal agencies to use them as supportive evidence.[12] Thus, when the data from other sources are debatable, the results of short-term tests can be influential in policy decisions. But in practice, most information needed for hazard identification comes from studies on laboratory animals.

Environmental Toxicology

In animal studies, toxicologists give laboratory rats—or mice or guinea pigs or some other mammals—huge doses of a suspect chemical, and when the animals die they examine their organs for abnormalities. The studies usually take two years and follow a routine protocol. One group of fifty males and fifty females receives the maximum dose the animals will tolerate without becoming sick. A second group of fifty males and fifty females receives a lower dose. A third group, which is given none of the chemical, serves as a control. Whether the animals get their dose in food, have it painted on their skin, or inhale it depends on what toxicologists think the usual route of exposure is for humans. Whether the results of the studies are deemed positive or negative depends on the difference between the responses of the test animals and the responses of the controls.

The use of animal bioassays rests on the idea that the effect of a chemical on laboratory animals is similar to its effect on humans. Thus, the reasoning goes, what one learns from animal studies can be extrapolated to humans. It is usually the case, however, that *any* effect on either humans or animals is relatively rare, so one cannot learn much of anything by exposing only a few hundred animals. At least one cannot learn much from exposing a few hundred animals to the small amount of the chemical that humans routinely encounter. The only way to effectively test the chemical, short of giving low doses to hundreds of thousands of rats at a cost of millions of dollars for each chemical, is to administer high doses to a few animals.

The problem comes in the extrapolations from animals to humans, and from high to low doses. Are humans really as sensitive to chemicals as laboratory animals are? And what actually happens when animals or humans are exposed to low doses? It is impossible to come up with a confident answer to the first question because not all animals are equally sensitive to chemicals. Take two examples: mice and rats develop cancer when exposed to methylene chloride, but hamsters do not.[13] Monkeys, dogs, and hamsters get cancer from exposure to 2-naphthylamine, but rats and rabbits do not.[14] Moreover, different species of animals, exposed to the same chemical, may develop tumors in different organs. There are even differences between the way males and females of the same species react to chemical tests. For example, male rats develop kidney tumors when exposed to several chemicals, but female rats exposed to these same chemicals do not.[15]

The extrapolation from animals to humans is further complicated by not knowing whether humans are more sensitive to a particular chemical compound than animals or less sensitive. The cases for which data on humans exist show a wide variation. Dioxin, which is routinely called the most toxic carcinogen ever tested, causes liver cancer in female rats exposed to 10 nanograms per kilogram of body weight per day (a nanogram is one billionth of a gram),[16] but all the data on humans suggest that people can tolerate considerably higher doses before being harmed.[17] In contrast, thalidomide, which can induce birth defects in humans at a dosage of half a milligram per kilogram of body weight per day, has no effect on female dogs unless they get over a hundred milligrams per kilogram of body weight per day.[18]

Another difficulty in extrapolating from animals to humans arises because the administered dose may be different from the received dose. Bodily processes, it turns out, can modulate the toxicologist's carefully measured chemical in unpredictable ways. For example, the liver produces enzymes that can detoxify some materials circulating in the blood, rendering them harmless. Conversely, metabolism can transform some fairly benign substances into more toxic ones. Moreover, these detoxification and activation processes can occur simultaneously in the same or in different organs.[19] Such complex mechanisms muddle the whole concept of dose even when it is applied only to animal testing.

The EPA has solved the extrapolation problem posed by such findings by simply ruling that humans are as sensitive as the most sensitive animal species, strain, or sex.[20] That ruling begs a lot of questions; furthermore it is a policy decision, not a scientific conclusion. It helps regulators get on with their job; it does not help them or anyone else to know whether a given chemical is actually dangerous to humans.

Extrapolating from high to low doses, too, depends more on political judgment than on scientific data. Animal bioassays produce an incomplete dose-response curve. Instead of starting where the dose and response axes meet, it starts at a point where both dose and response are high. The question is what shape the curve (or line) would take if there were data on the response to low doses. The line could be straight, bisecting perfectly the dose and response axes. Such a line would indicate that there is no safe dosage and that each increased dose brings a proportionate increased response. On the other hand, the line that started where the dose and response axes meet could curve like a hockey stick and lie along the horizontal dose axis for some distance. Such a line would indicate that there is a threshold below which exposure to a substance is safe. A third possibility is that the whacking part of the hockey stick could dip somewhat below the dose axis. Such a curve would indicate that exposure is beneficial at low doses.[21]

Given these possible configurations, and indeed many more, the EPA chooses a straight linear model. That is, where no data exist to show the actual response at low doses but animal tests show that a substance causes cancer at high doses, the EPA's policy is to assume that even the smallest exposure is dangerous to humans and that every increase in dosage results in a corresponding increase in response. In animal studies of noncarcinogens, the EPA takes the highest exposure shown to have no adverse effects and then adds an "uncertainty factor." Or, more precisely, the EPA *divides* the animal dosage by ten or a hundred or a thousand in setting safe exposure for humans. What uncertainty factor the EPA uses depends primarily on whether it thinks the animal studies are of low, medium, or high quality.[22]

Both the reliance on a linear model and the use of an uncertainty factor seek to protect public health, and in that sense they are good policies. But they are only policies. They are not statements about the actual effects on people of exposure to the chemicals. Animal studies simply cannot deliver that information. There is a clear scientific rationale for the policy: almost all known human carcinogens are also carcinogenic in at least one animal species. But there are far fewer data on humans than on animals, and there is no way to know the number of exceptions to the rule.

So we have a paradox. Animal tests have an important function in risk assessment: they provide scientific data on the health hazards of chemicals. But the data the tests provide are not what risks assessors need to know. The EPA circumvents the paradox and makes the data usable by adopting two policy assumptions. One assumption is that human response to toxins is similar to the response of the most vulnerable laboratory animals. The other assumption is that animals' reaction to large doses directly predicts their reaction to small ones. Neither assumption is scientific; both are policy decisions. Together they help support strict environmental policies and citizen opposition to chemical waste. They also make every environmental risk assessment vulnerable to the charge that the information on which it is built—the information gathered in the initial two steps—is imprecise at best and downright wrong at worst.[23]

Environmental Epidemiology

Because animal studies cannot reveal how humans actually respond to environmental exposures, it might seem that risk assessors would put more store in environmental epidemiology. Environmental epidemiologists study the health effects of pollution on humans. They go into areas where the air or water or soil is polluted with industrial waste and try to learn whether the residents' health problems are linked to the pollution. This task is so difficult, however, that environmental epidemiologists usually cannot provide much indisputable information for risk assessment either. In fact, risk assessors seldom use data from epidemiological research. Some epidemiologists do argue that risk assessments would be more accurate if they included environmental epidemiology.[24] But others say that, because epidemiological studies are so frequently unable to show a correlation between pollution and disease, using them only exacerbates the problems of assessing risk from animal data.[25] To explain the controversy, I discuss three major difficulties environmental epidemiologists face: identifying disease, proving validity, and getting exposure data.

Identifying Disease. One enduring problem is finding out what the health problems are. The main way to learn about people's current or past illnesses is to interview them or ask their doctors. Unfortunately, information gathered from interviews is not particularly dependable. People's recall of their illnesses and miscarriages is notoriously inaccurate in the best of times,[26] and their accounts are even less reliable during periods of community turmoil over environmental exposures.[27] People are more likely to remember former bouts of illness, or to recall mild diseases as serious ones, when everyone in the community is talking about the contaminated water or the polluted air than when there is no such public issue. Because professional reseachers understand that people's perceptions are colored by context, the health information Lois Gibbs got by going from door to door at Love Canal never figured in a formal scientific study and the health data in the study on childhood illnesses came under fire. That is also why in Alsea, when the EPA researchers set out to corroborate Bonnie Hill's information on miscarriages, they went to hospital medical records.

Yet hospital records are not always a good source of information, either. For one thing, they are hard to find. People's medical records can be scattered among many providers, inside and outside hospitals, over a large geographic area. And even if they are found, there can be legal and ethical barriers to epidemiologists who want to read them. If these hurdles are overcome, going through pages and pages of medical reports is extremely costly in terms of time and money. Only specially trained people can make sense of medical codes and language. In addition, because a variety of physicians with differing kinds of interests and training and expertise write them, the records will not be uniform, nor will they include every condition or symptom that, in retrospect, seems relevant to chemical exposures. Many conditions, in fact, will be missed simply because they were never brought to a health professional in the first place. Miscarriages, so frequently of concern to people exposed to environmental pollution, are the premier case in point. Finally, little quirky things can make reliance on medical records difficult. At Love Canal, investigator Beverly Paigen and her colleagues could not get the medical records of residents for their study of childhood illnesses because the New York Department of Health was using them for its own Love Canal investigation.[28]

The most reliable medical information comes from the big data banks for birth defects and cancer kept by state health departments. Environmental epidemiologists can simply consult a central data bank if they suspect that exposure to a pollutant has had reproductive or carcinogenic effects. But here too, there are problems. Not all states keep birth defect data banks. In those that do, some hospitals do not comply with the reporting requirement; the coding of congenital malformations is not uniform from hospital to hospital; and certain congenital malformations are not identifiable at birth.[29] The usefulness of cancer registries is limited by the fact that cancer has a long latency period. Twenty, thirty, and in some cases as many as forty years can pass between the time of exposure to a carcinogen and the development of a malignant tumor. So, often, when scientists study a community soon after environmental contamination has been discovered, the population has not had time to develop the cancers that exposure might cause. Consequently, even a community whose health has been affected by exposure to a carcinogen or group of carcinogens may have a health profile quite similar to an unexposed community's. That health profile might change significantly in time, but until the change actually takes place, epidemiological studies devoted to cancer will be negative.

The Love Canal cancer study provides an example. Done in 1981, about three years after authorities had discovered that the landfill was leaking, the study could not be expected to detect the cancers that exposure to the leachate could cause. The authors of the study knew this, of course. They duly reminded readers that "questions of long latency periods cannot yet be addressed," and most supporters of the Love Canal protests who comment on the absence of elevated cancer rates there note the same problem.[30] Even opponents of environmental activism acknowledge it. Elizabeth Whelan—who calls Love Canal "a classic story of half truths, distorted historical facts, unprecedented media exaggeration, and misguided government intervention"—says about the cancer study, "because of the long latencies involved, this finding does not rule out the possibility that cancer may appear in the future."[31]

Proving Validity. In addition to the difficulties of discovering health problems, epidemiologists run into all sorts of trouble making sense of the ones they do find. The point, after all, is not simply to generate a list of diseases or miscarriages, but to link those problems with environmental pollution. That is hard to do unless confounding factors are successfully ruled out. A community may be located on top of a Superfund site and suffer from many cancers or birth defects or childhood illnesses. But maybe people there smoke a lot, or are exposed to toxic chemicals at work, or are simply poor. These factors are all correlated with disease. The environmental epidemiologist has to figure out how to measure such variables and how to determine their contribution to the community's health problems. But since no one knows for sure how to do either task completely accurately, whatever conclusion the epidemiologist comes to will be uncertain.[32]

Environmental epidemiologists also have to show that a disease profile is unusual. The community on the Superfund site may have many health problems unexplained by smoking or by exposure to occupational toxins. Yet, if these health problems differ little from those in similar communities without pollution, as is frequently the case, epidemiologists cannot say that the pollution caused them. The Love Canal studies on cancer and reproductive problems provide good examples; so does the Connecticut Department of Health Service's study on cancers in Guilford. And critics of grassroots mobilizing eagerly point out others.[33] Complicating the issue even further is the fact that sometimes, even when a community's diseases cannot be explained away by confounding factors and even when the community has a clear excess number of diseases compared with controls, attributing the diseases to pollution is impossible because epidemiologists must show that their data are statistically significant.

The rule for statistical significance is exceedingly strict: research results must have a likelihood of no more than 5 percent of occurring by chance. Put another way, investigators must be 95 percent confident that the sample they have studied represents the real world. The statistical likelihood is derived from standard mathematical tests.[34] This high standard prevents epidemiologists from claiming they have found an excess of disease when in fact they have not. Yet in very small populations the rule also can prevent them from detecting health risks even when they exist.

Imagine that a community is exposed to a toxic substance at levels that could cause one in 10,000 people to die from cancer. (This would pose a serious public health hazard. The EPA's express policy is that exposure must be reduced if more than one in a million excess cancer deaths would occur.[35]) In a small city of 100,000 people that would mean 10 extra cancer deaths each year. But cancer is a fairly common disease. In the United States, it accounts for about 20 percent of all deaths annually—or, given an overall death rate of 872.4 per 100,000 people, an average of around 175 deaths per year in a city of 100,000. The actual number will vary from year to year. Ten extra cancer deaths in that city could not be distinguished from the expected variation. And it would not be statistically significant at the 95 percent confidence level.

In a much smaller community, such as the few thousand or even few hundred people typically exposed to the water or air or soil around a hazardous waste site, the problem of detecting excess death rates is worse. Say an epidemiologist studies a community with about five thousand people, like Love Canal. A carcinogen that could kill one person in every ten thousand might not cause even one excess death in a population of only five thousand people. So the problem is not that extra deaths occur but that they are statistically nonsignificant. The problem is that, given the odds, no extra deaths are likely to occur, even though the substance in question may be highly toxic. A community that small would have to have an extraordinary number of cancer deaths for the effect of exposure to the carcinogen to be deemed statistically significant—more deaths over a decade, calculates one epidemiologist, than eight times the expected number.[36] As the authors of the Love Canal cancer study remarked blandly, "The small size of the study population limit[s] the findings of epidemiological studies of this type."[37]

As we have seen, however, small communities have, in fact, experienced the high number of excess deaths or diseases necessary for statistical significance. One of these was—or at least initially appeared to be—Meadow Street in Guilford. The other was Alsea. Such events are called "clusters," and they make health departments uneasy because clusters may represent exactly what communities think they do: high levels of harmful environmental pollutants. On the other hand, they may represent what health departments hope they do: ordinary patterns of variation in disease distribution.

To understand how epidemiologists think of clusters, imagine a little boy inexpertly throwing darts at a big map of the United States. (Put him outside, behind the garage.) Let's say he has thousands of darts in many different colors, each one representing a different disease. When he's finished, the darts will be spread out all over the map, but some will likely cluster in certain places. So there might be a clump of green ones in a little town in Virginia, representing, say, meningitis, and a lot of orange ones massed together in the northeastern corner of Colorado, representing melanomas. And in some places there could be a tight bunch of darts in all colors. The clusters clearly exist, yet they're scientifically meaningless; they're due to pure chance.

With this concept in mind, health department officials are likely to greet reports of disease clusters with questions. Are the diseases in the cluster all of the same type? Has the cluster persisted over time? If environmental contamination *is* present, have people actually been exposed to it?[38]

The first question, about homogeneity, came up in Guilford, where neighbors reported five brain cancers on Meadow Street's one block. The chief epidemiologist for the state of Connecticut, David Brown, examined the state's tumor registry and reported that of the five cases on the street, one was actually a melanoma of the eye and one was an esophageal cancer that had metastasized to the brain. The remaining three were all brain cancers, but one was probably caused by head injuries.[39] On this evidence, Brown concluded that there was no cluster of brain cancers on Meadow Street. He was proceeding under the rule that cancer is not one disease but many diseases, each with its own cause. From an epidemiological perspective these cancers are no more related to one another than are say, AIDS, pyelonephritis, and asthma. The types of cancer on Meadow Street have no known etiologic agent in common, so finding them all on one block did not signify a public health emergency.

The second question, about persistence, came up in Alsea, where residents and then the EPA found a cluster of miscarriages. For epidemiologists the question in such cases is whether the miscarriages follow the herbicide spraying. If they do sometimes but not other times, then investigators attribute a grouping of miscarriages to chance. Thus, scientists at Oregon State University who reviewed the EPA data announced that a cluster did exist in Alsea but it was meaningless because it was only a one-time occurrence. In the previous few years, when spraying had also occurred, no unusual number of women had miscarried. In their words,

> The seasonal cyclic peaks seen by EPA in the six-year cumulative data are consistent with a model of random variation. The data are highly variable from area to area and from year to year. The "June peak" in the Study area occurred only in one year of the six-year study and should not be presented as a repetitive event.[40]

The third question, about exposures, is so much more complex than the other two that it deserves separate consideration. It should have separate consideration anyway because in the risk assessment process, exposure assessment constitutes the critical third step.

Getting Exposure Data. Even if great numbers of people living near a hazardous waste dump or breathing polluted air have cancer or suffer miscarriages, epidemiologists cannot attribute the health problems to a polluted environment unless they know the extent to which people have come into contact with it. Getting that information is not at all easy to do, especially in contrast with the task toxicologists have. For toxicologists, working in laboratories, exposure information is easy to come by. Unless they are sloppy record keepers or careless animal attendants, they know precisely what amounts of which chemical have been given to which animals for how long by which route. For epidemiologists, investigating a possible Superfund site or disease cluster, all that information is hidden. To uncover it, they have to figure out some way to measure things they cannot manipulate, namely "the contaminate, its source, the environmental media of exposure, avenues of transport through each medium, chemical and physical transformations, routes of entry into the body, intensity and frequency of contact, and its spatial and temporal concentration patterns."[41]

There is not room in this chapter to discuss all the measurement problems that long list implies.[42] But I will comment on the last two items: the intensity and frequency of a community's contact with the contaminant and the contaminant's spatial and temporal concentration patterns. Consider a subdivision along an abandoned landfill where leachate from the fill has seeped into the groundwater and contaminated the drinking water in people's wells. How do you measure the residents' contact with the leachate? Some people may not have been actually exposed to much of the water. They might always drink bottled water and mainly eat food prepared in restaurants across town near their workplace. Those who do drink the water and eat most meals at home probably have all been exposed to unequal amounts of the pollutant, depending on their individual or household habits. Or consider a group of houses sitting near a waste incinerator's smokestack. Some people in those houses are usually away at work; others seldom leave the neighborhood. Of those who stay home, some spend most of their time indoors; others are outside much of the day.

Epidemiologists wanting know if exposure to the pollutants could be responsible for disease in the community need these kinds of details on individual people's lives. But given the difficulty of getting them accurately, even the most careful household surveys are likely to misclassify people. The misclassification will bias the research results. For example, if a sample of apparently exposed people unwittingly includes many who are actually unexposed, researchers are unlikely to find a correlation between exposure and disease. This would occur even if the exposed people have unusually high rates of health problems and the unexposed people do not, for the misclassified people "dilute" the study.

Gathering accurate data on the contaminant's spatial and temporal concentration presents similar difficulties and can create similar biases. Even if everybody in the community drinks exactly the same quantity of well water (adjusted for body weight), different wells can have different levels of contamination. Some wells near a leaking landfill can even be uncontaminated, depending on the pathway of the underground plume. You are not measuring exposure to a pollutant by noting people's intake of water, unless you know their wells were actually polluted during the time they were drinking the water. By the same token, people who live near a hazardous waste incinerator may actually be exposed to fewer airborne toxins than are people who live farther from the incinerator, but downwind. Such information about pollutants might be relatively easy to obtain for current, ongoing contamination. It is far harder to learn about the past. Which wells might have been polluted five, ten, or twenty years ago? What was in the air at that time, and what were the usual wind patterns? To answer such questions epidemiological studies have to include hydrogeological information about the characteristics of soil and meteorological information about prevailing winds. Only with these data can they identify the appropriate subjects of their investigations. But they might get the wrong data.

The swale theory at Love Canal is a good example of the problem. When the leaks in the landfill were first discovered, health department officials assumed that residents living closest to the canal were at greatest risk. Hence they evacuated families in the first two rings of houses. Later, some of the older residents remembered that small streams once crisscrossed the area. The streams had long ago dried up and had been filled with rubble as builders put up new homes, but to many people it seemed reasonable that liquid spreading out from the canal would travel most easily via these underground "swales."[43] If that were so, the residents with the greatest exposure would not be those living near the canal but those living near the swales. And indeed, one study did find a correlation between childhood illness and exposure to the swales.[44] The principal author of the study had already said that the health department had erred in its earlier announcement that miscarriages at Love Canal were unrelated to chemical exposure; the department should have used swales, not distance from the canal, as the proxy for exposure.[45]

Critics reject the swale theory, saying that no one knows the precise location of the swales and no one has actually tested the ability of leachate to flow along them.[46] If these critics are right, the study on childhood illness may be questionable, and the decision to evacuate everyone from Love Canal becomes even less scientifically justifiable. On the other hand, if the swale theory does explain what happened at Love Canal, new study designs might result in positive research outcomes, not just for miscarriages but for other health problems as well. Or maybe there are other routes of exposure that epidemiologists did not think of. The lesson here, again, is that dependable exposure data are hard to get. With erroneous assumptions about the ways people come into contact with a pollutant, epidemiologists are unlikely to find a relation between pollution and health, even when one exists.

The EPA's search for clear risk assessments as an objective guide to policy is doomed to failure. The list of problems, as we have just seen, is long. Data on the relation between pollution and health are inherently obscure. Most of the information about cancer comes from animal studies, which may or may not reveal anything about the effect of chemicals on human beings. Data on the health problems of people in polluted communities are hard to get because of recall bias, the vagaries of medical records, and the long latency period before cancer develops. A link between health problems and pollution can seldom be established because there are so many confounding variables, because health differences between exposed communities and unexposed communities are hard to detect, because in small communities the data are rarely statistically significant, and because it is nearly impossible to get reliable exposure information. Few risk assessments, therefore, will be strong enough to support aggressive environmental policies. For the same reasons, risk assessments will probably fail to support the claim by members of grassroots environmental groups that their health is endangered from exposure to pollution. Some individual studies might show that exposure is hazardous, yet the overall research picture is unlikely to do so.

Viewing the claims of grassroots groups through the lens of science like this, one might conclude, as many people have, that, although citizen participation is desirable in general, citizens should be discouraged from trying to influence environmental policy decisions. After all, the science to support their claims is just not there. That conclusion, however, represents a misunderstanding about science. Science is not a product. It is a tool. Or, more accurately, science is a huge collection of many different kinds of tools used for investigating the world. Some tools are very good. They are finely crafted and well-suited for the job at hand: for example, the toneometers that ophthalmologists use for discovering glaucoma. Some tools are quite poor. They are crudely designed and ill-suited for the job at hand: for example, the little sticks or toothpicks that children sometimes use for exploring insect anatomy. The tools in the environmental health sciences are not really analogous to toothpicks, but the animal bioassays, cancer registries, questionnaires, and statistical formulas that researchers use to understand the relationship between pollution and health are closer to the toothpick end of the scale than to the toneometer end.

Unfortunately, no one has devised better tools for this job. However, what is available can be used differently. In fact, what is available *is* being used differently. Increasingly, as I show in Chapter Four, environmental scientists are designing studies that enable them to demonstrate links between exposure to environmental pollution and disease. These changes in science follow upon and are, in an important sense, consistent with ideas about nature that environmentalists began promoting in the 1960s. The next chapter, therefore, is about those ideas and the impact they have had on the general public's beliefs and values.

3 New Ideas about Nature

In Chapter Two, I ask why scientists have such a hard time linking exposure to disease. In this chapter, I ask why it seems so sensible to most of us that communities should be protected from exposure to industrial wastes when peer-reviewed studies by reputable investigators have failed to show clear correlations between pollution and disease. The question is reasonable because until quite recently virtually no one thought industrial wastes were a public problem, despite their abundance. To answer the question, I point to the environmental movement's efforts over the past thirty years to develop and promote a new view of nature.

Pre-environmentalism

Anyone who was politically conscious before the mid-1960s can remember the pre-environmentalist era. Until about that time there was no talk about an environmental crisis. Nature did not seem to be in need of protection. Water pollution was something one encountered only in the Third World. Air pollution was an accepted part of industrialization.[1] Children used to run behind the trucks that sprayed DDT, playing in the fog.[2] Development projects that dammed rivers, drained marshes, and turned farmlands into subdivisions were everywhere hailed as progress. Without thinking about it much one way or another, most people assumed they could throw their garbage "out." Not only the school at Love Canal but also other schools were built on hazardous waste sites without protest from the public.[3] Glass producers could boast to customers that their bottles were not returnable. A plywood company could run an ad declaring: "200

Year Old Redwood Forests Prove the Durability of Malarky Redwood Plywood."[4] Newspapers and news magazines had no environmental beat; legislators had no environmental staff people.[5] A nuclear reactor could have a partial meltdown without causing public protest.[6] A common slogan among engineers was, "The solution to pollution is dilution." Cancer patients did not intuit that pollution caused their health problems.

Environmental scholars today partly account for these ways of thinking by noting the hegemony of the Cartesian idea that nature is like a machine. The idea made it possible to conceptually separate humans from nature and to treat plants and animals as no more than mechanical objects. From a Cartesian perspective, nature is simply raw material for human progress. It is a means to a end. In the words of Donald Worster: "By reducing plants and animals to insensate matter, mere conglomerates of atomic particles devoid of internal purpose or intelligence, the [follower of Descartes] was removing the remaining barriers to unrestrained economic exploitation."[7]

Environmental scholars also remind us, however, that those ideas predate Descartes. They show up in the first chapter of Genesis, when God tells Adam and Eve, "Be fruitful and multiply, and fill the earth and subdue it; and have dominion over the fish of the sea and over the birds of the air and over every living thing that moves upon the earth."[8] The belief that humans were put on the earth to rule over nature characterized classical Greek and early Christian cultures. It was accepted unquestioningly throughout the middle ages. It supported the Reformation and the beginnings of industrialization.[9]

The utilitarian views of nature lay behind Jeremy Bentham's appraisal of North America at the end of the eighteenth century:

> Savage nature may be seen there, side by side with civilized nature. The interior of that immense region offers only a frightful solitude, impenetrable forests or sterile plains, stagnant waters and impure vapours; such is the earth when left to itself.... But on the borders of these frightful solitudes, what different sights are to be seen! We appear to comprehend in the same view the two empires of good and evil. Forests give place to cultivated fields; morasses are dried up, and the surface, grown firm, is covered with meadows, pastures, domestic animals, habitations healthy and smiling.[10]

And utilitarian views informed a speech by a mid-nineteenth-century U.S. Congressman who warned, "Unless the government shall grant head rights or donations of some kind, these prairies... will for centuries continue to be the home of the wild deer and wolf; their stillness will be undisturbed by the jocund song of the farmer, and their deep and fertile soil unbroken by the ploughshare. Something must be done to remedy this evil."[11]

Of course, not everyone assumed that nature had only use value. Many nineteenth-century naturalists argued, along with Darwin, that plants and animals could not be analyzed in terms that separated them from humans. The assertion received a name in 1866 when Ernst Haeckel, a German zoologist, coined the term *ecology*. It was considerably advanced in the 1890s by Eugenius Warming in Denmark and Frederic Clements in Nebraska. Each of these men, reasoning that nature is more like a living organism than a machine, described natural habitats as progressing toward a "climax." This is a pivotal concept in ecology, referring, in Donald Worster's words, to "nothing less than the most diverse, stable, well-balanced, self-perpetuating society that can be devised.... "[12] Later investigators, employing concepts such as "web of life," "ecosystem," and "biotic community" further developed ecology, establishing it as a branch of science that opposed Cartesian dualism and focused instead on the patterns and relationships in whole systems.[13]

From the beginning, the new science of ecology shared some of its logic with that of peoples, and individuals, who held the natural world as sacred—a view of nature most famously promoted in the nineteenth century by Henry David Thoreau and John Muir. Both men preached against the old views. They said nature should be honored and cherished, for it is the source of wisdom, solace, and virtue. Thoreau wrote, "The earth I tread on is not a dead, inert mass; it is a body, has a spirit, is organic and fluid to the influence of its spirit." He raged against Concord farmers who treated land like mere property, writing that some farmers "deserve to be prosecuted for maltreating the face of nature committed to their care."[14] And Muir, after encountering Yosemite's waterfalls for the first time, marveled that the "water does not seem to be under the dominion of ordinary [Newtonian] laws, but rather as if it were a living creature, full of the strength of the mountains and their huge wild joy." He later lamented, "How narrow we selfish, conceited creatures are in our sympathies! How blind to the rights of all the rest of creation!"[15]

Environmentalist Principles

Despite the familiarity of these sentiments today, until the middle of the twentieth century they were eccentric in Western cultures. The average person's views of nature reflected neither the science of ecology nor the moralizing of Thoreau and Muir. To be sure, ecology was taught in universities [16] and both the Sierra Club (which was largely Muir's creation) and the National Audubon Society were familiar organizations. But the ecological concept of nature as interconnected was mainly a way for scientists to organize the study of plants and animals. And, although, the idea that nature is intrinsically valuable had poetic resonance, it served primarily to justify protecting specific wilderness areas from development. In everyday discourse "the environment" was not a conceptual category with any social meaning.[17]

Then, starting in the early 1960s a handful of new visionaries and their supporters—writing books and articles, giving seminars and speeches—began promoting the idea we know today as environmentalism. They took the ecological principle that people should not interfere in the balance of nature and the ethical principle that nature should be exalted and added a political principle. They argued that all of nature is seriously endangered and that we must change our values and our institutions in order to save it. This was a radical new concept. Thoreau and his followers had urged people to develop a more reverential attitude toward nature, but the goal was more to benefit people—to restore their souls—than to safeguard nature for its own sake. Muir and his followers had linked reverence for nature with the insistence that nature should be protected, but only certain places in nature were at issue. The ideas of the ecologists had much broader implications, yet the ecologists conducted themselves like any other group of scientists. They did not take on the role of public ethicists. In their view, the applications of their work were for resource managers and farmers.[18] So environmentalism was something novel. Saying that all of nature is endangered assigned new meaning to the ecological and ethical principles, giving them urgency. Together the three principles provided the moral basis for a new social movement, the first one in history based not on people's relations to one another but on people's relations to nature.

The list of environmentalism's chief creators starts with Rachel Carson, who published *Silent Spring* in 1962, and it includes Barry Commoner (*Science and Survival,* 1963), Aldo Leopold (*A Sand County Almanac,* 1966), Murray Bookchin (*Our Synthetic Environment,* 1962), and René Dubos (*Man Adapting,* 1965). Over and over, these writers described grave ecological consequences from releasing pesticides and industrial waste into the air, land, and water and from giving land over to tourism and development. They asserted that treating nature instrumentally is immoral. And they declared that unless we make drastic changes, life as we know it could come to an end.

Rachel Carson wrote as a scientist, emphasizing ecology and primarily describing the wide effects on nature and humans of synthetic pesticides. What makes her a founder of environmentalism is that she gave these scientific principles both ethical and political significance. *Silent Spring* was a treatise on the interconnectedness of nature; it laid out in dramatic detail the far-reaching consequences of using artificial pesticides on crops. Yet it was more than a book about what farmers do. It was a book about what "we" do. The book's aim was to get the general population, not simply farmers, to change their understanding of nature.

Throughout the book, Carson portrayed ecological principles not only in terms of true and false but also in terms of right and wrong. She did it by using language signaling that the standards ethical people apply to the treatment of humans apply also to the treatment of other living things. The "unselective bludgeon of insecticidal poisons," Carson said, creates "casualty lists" and "chemical warfare." It "dooms" plants and animals which "fall victim" and are "stricken," to "annihilation." She pleaded with readers to consider "the cat beloved of some family, the farmer's cattle, the rabbit in the field, and the horned lark out of the sky. These creatures are innocent of any harm to man. Indeed by their very existence they and their fellows make life more pleasant. Yet he rewards them with a death that is not only sudden but horrible." She asked, "By acquiescing in an act that can cause such suffering to a living creature, who among us is not diminished as a human being?"[19]

Along with the moral lesson, Carson urged political action. "Who has made the decision," she demanded, "that sets in motion these chains of poisonings, this ever-widening wave of death that spreads out, like ripples when a pebble is dropped into a still pond?" Her answer was less than precise about the decision maker, but it was clear about who had the ultimate responsibility: "The decision is that of the authoritarian temporarily entrusted with power; he has made it during a moment of inattention by millions to whom beauty and the ordered world of nature still have a meaning that is deep and imperative." In other words, people who care about nature's beauty and order must scrutinize those who hold political power and pressure them to act differently. Her final chapter described some of the non-chemical ways to control insects developed by local and national agriculture departments around the world. "The choice," she said, between destructive chemicals and these alternatives, "is ours to make."[20]

If Rachel Carson's argument was grounded in ecology and moved on to ethics and politics, Aldo Leopold's was grounded in ethics and moved on to politics and ecology. One reason Leopold is less well known than Carson is that he brought the three elements of environmentalism together in only one short section of *A Sand County Almanac*, but it was an influential section, precisely because it implied radical social action. Most of the book consisted of lyrical paeans to plants, animals, and the changing of the seasons. They were lovely essays, but they were the stuff of poetry and of religion, not the stuff of social movements. They inspired reverence in readers, not collective action. What gives Leopold his place as a creator of the environmental movement is his concept of a "land ethic."

In laying out this concept, Leopold switched from simply describing nature's wonders to warning readers that unless they develop an ethical attitude toward nature, the beauty of nature will be destroyed. It was an explicit call for an entirely new moral code. He compared humans' use of nature for their own ends to the practice of slavery. "There is yet no ethic dealing with man's relation to the land and to the plants and animals which grow upon it," he said, but it is "an evolutionary possibility and an ecological necessity." He insisted that animals and plants have as much right to exist as do humans and, that, like humans, their value is intrinsic. In a moral world, he said, the value of nonhumans would have nothing to do with their economic worth. He declared that "a land ethic changes the role of *Homo sapiens* from conqueror of the land-community to plain member and citizen of it. It implies respect for the community as such."[21]

So, whereas Carson based her call for action on a story about the inevitable effect of pesticides on all living things, Leopold based his call on a story about the intrinsic similarity between nature and humans. As did Carson, Leopold implored his readers to understand nature as being interconnected. Nature, he said consists of "a tangle of chains so complex as to seem disorderly, yet the stability of the system proves it to be a highly organized structure. Its functioning depends on the co-operation and competition of its diverse parts." And he, too, warned about interfering with nature. "[M]an-made changes are of a different order than evolutionary changes, and have effects more comprehensive than is intended or foreseen."[22] But Leopold's primary message was moral. We must change our ideas about nature not just because misusing it has consequences, but because the natural world, like human beings, has inherent worth.

The other creators of environmentalism in the 1960s similarly combined ecological, ethical, and political messages. In *Science and Survival,* Barry Commoner argued that to develop technology without considering its ecological consequences is suicidal. The only salvation is a new system of morality. "In recent times the gap between traditional moral principles and the realities of modern life has become so large as to precipitate... urgent demands for renewal—for the development of statements of moral purpose which are directly relevant to the modern world."[23]

Murray Bookchin's argument was that environmental degradation is an inevitable result of unfettered industrial capitalism. He connected cancer, coronary disease, and respiratory illnesses to modern agricultural and industrial practices, concentrating particularly on pesticide use and the release of radiation into the environment. His underlying thesis was that plants, animals, and the soil exist in a delicate and complex web of relationships and that industrialization, with its built-in concepts of hierarchy and domination, is destroying the web. "It is not within the realm of fantasy to suggest that if the breakdown of the soil cosmos continues unabated, if plant and animal health continue to deteriorate, if insect infestations multiply, and if chemical controls become increasingly lethal, many of the preconditions for advanced life will be irreparably damaged and the earth will become incapable of supporting a viable, healthy human species."[24]

René Dubos, too, wrote about nature's intricate web. *Man Adapting* was a long and detailed attack against reductionism. He argued that we cannot understand health and disease without coming to grips with the interplay among all living things. In a prescient chapter he asserted that Rachel Carson had focused too narrowly, that chemical pesticides were only one of many environmental pollutants, "probably the least important." He said we must also be concerned about all the "varied and unpredictable... dangers of modern technology." Among the dangers he listed are the estrogens fed to cattle, the increasing exposures to lead, and worsening water and air pollution. He ridiculed the belief that new synthetic organic compounds discharged into rivers will be rendered harmless by a "purifying process" and said that the frequent poisoning of aquatic life demonstrates the impurity of drinking water. He discussed a whole panoply of air pollutants and said that often the problem is not any particular pollutant but a complex combination.[25]

The most concise articulation of environmentalist ideas is in Barry Commoner's 1971 book *The Closing Circle.* There he argued that if we are to survive the ecological crisis we must embrace the four "Laws of Ecology." The first law, said Commoner, is that everything is connected to everything else; the earth is an elaborate ecosystem whose interconnecting parts form a network of multiple causes and effects. Complex feedback loops, food chains, and periodic fluctuations within the system and its subsystems are so delicately balanced that "a small perturbation in one place may have large, distant, long-delayed effects" in another. The second law is that everything must go somewhere; there is no "away." We may think that we have thrown something "out," but in reality "it is simply transferred from place to place, converted from one molecular form to another, acting on the life process of any organism in which it becomes, for a time, lodged." The third law is that nature knows best; over the eons of evolution, dysfunctional organisms and ecosystems have been weeded out, so to speak, and only those with compatible parts have survived. In this sense, nature is not perfectible. The best already exists. Any new "major man-made change in a natural system is likely to be *detrimental* to that system." Finally, there is no free lunch. "Because the ecosystem is a connected whole, in which nothing can be gained or lost and which is not subject to over-all improvement, anything extracted from it by human effort must be replaced."[26]

These four environmental principles, the Laws of Ecology, were fostered by many voices in the 1960s. The voices included university faculty and administrators; journalists working for newspapers and news magazines; radio and television personalities; legislators at all levels of government; bureaucrats and consultants in the fields of urban planning, development, agriculture, and energy; heads of charitable foundations; and the clergy.[27]

In addition, untold numbers of social activists promoted the environmentalist message in the 1960s. Some were members of the old conservationist organizations such as the Sierra Club, the National Wildlife Federation, and the National Audubon Society. Others were members of a new environmentalist organization, the Environmental Defense Fund.[28] Protesters against atomic testing also fostered environmentalist principles when they argued that radioactive fallout moves up the food chain and concentrates toxicity at each link. Supporters of Zero Population Growth used environmentalist imagery, maintaining that overpopulation threatened our fragile planet. Fishermen and farmers trying to get the government to control surface mining emphasized its ecological effects on water quality and agricultural lands. And all across the country, groups of citizens rebroadcast Rachel Carson's message about the interconnectedness of nature as they fought to restrict the use of DDT.[29]

Environmentalist principles were also promoted in the sweeping critique of dominant social values that characterized the 1960s. Civil rights activists, antiwar activists, and feminists used envirionmentalist principles to reinforce their demands for a more egalitarian society, one in which all people live together in harmony. Counterculturalists emphasized environmentalism with their vision for a decentralized, less-materialistic society, in which people live in small communities, close to the land, using as few resources as possible. Socialists and Marxists drew on environmentalism to explain the desirability of a truly democratic order, one guided not by industrial capitalism's need for growth but by people's need for one another.[30]

Environmentalist principles were most theatrically advanced on April 22, 1970—the first Earth Day. Some twenty million people attended public events that day to demonstrate their conviction that nature is interconnected, existing in harmonious balance when undisturbed by humans; that nature has inherent worth and cannot ethically be used for human ends; and that nature is endangered and must be saved.

Of course, the men and women I refer to did not promote environmentalist ideas in the abstract. Actual events in the 1960s supported them. Air pollution in many industrial areas got noticeably worse. Two large oil spills occurred, one in Santa Barbara and one in the English Channel. The Cuyahoga River caught fire. The Bureau of Reclamation announced plans to dam the Colorado River and flood portions of the Grand Canyon. In upstate New York, Con Edison tried to build a hydroelectric plant at the base of Storm King mountain. These events, however, have no intrinsic social or political meaning. Nor have they any inherent relation to one another. When similar events had occurred before the 1960s, the media covered them as disparate occurrences. Foul air, oil spills, polluted rivers, disappearing canyons, and new hydroelectric plants did not illustrate any overarching social problem. (Indeed, as we have seen, stories about constructing dams and hydroelectric plants were for a long time simply about progress.) So the occurrence of these events in the 1960s did not prompt environmentalism. Instead, environmentalist principles gave them new meaning. The principles provided a new lens through which to view them. They provided a way of seeing each event as part of a larger phenomenon. Each thus took on new significance as one of a series of threats to the integrity of nature. At the same time, each event supplied environmentalists with a new reason to argue that the all of nature is interconnected, violable, and endangered.

Controversy within Environmentalism

Importantly, however, environmentalism is not all of a piece. From the beginning there have been splits within the movement over the causes of environmental degradation. In the late 1970s and again in the late 1980s new activists added ideas to environmentalism that fit awkwardly with the original principles. And, more recently, scholars sympathetic to the movement have given environmentalist thought much more critical examination than it received in the sixties.

One split in environmentalist ranks is the division, common to all social movements, between liberals and radicals. The two sides have been called "shallow ecologists" and "deep ecologists," as well as "light greens" and "dark greens." People on both sides advocate the basic environmentalist principles, but the liberal camp believes that the environmental crisis can be solved without major social change; the radical camp disagrees. There is also a different kind of split. This one divides the radicals into "ecocentrists" and "anthropocentrists" or, as some people put it, "deep ecologists" and "social ecologists." Both camps distinguish themselves from liberals. The salient difference between the two groups of radicals is their assignment of responsibility for environmental degradation.[31]

People in the ecocentrist/deep ecology camp emphasize personal accountability.[32] Inspired by Thoreau, Muir, and Leopold, this camp blames the environmental crisis primarily on the public's refusal to recognize humans' essential oneness with nature, to be humble in the face of nature's complexity, and to adopt a simple lifestyle in harmony with nature's rhythms. Arne Naess, the father of deep ecology, says he admires people who do environmental policy work, but "the best way to promote good causes is to provide a good example."[33] He urges people to live joyously in nature and to develop "self-realization" by constantly trying to understand their "ecological self." Promoting Naess's philosophy, Bill Devall and George Sessions also emphasize the centrality of personal transformation. They write that to halt the environmental crisis people must cultivate an "ecological consciousness" that makes them aware of the "balance and harmony between individuals, communities and all of Nature."[34]

In contrast, people in the anthropocentric/social ecology camp lay primary blame for the environmental crisis on the political economy.[35] A major spokesperson for this camp, Murray Bookchin, agrees with the need for new ways of thinking about nature, but he says that deep ecology courts misanthropy, fascism, and victim blaming. Saving nature, he insists, "will depend . . . on the extent to which countless social oppressions are permitted to exist that compel peasants to cut down forests in order to survive, and that destroy their traditional lifeways in the bargain."[36] Bookchin argues that industrial capitalism is the cause of environmental degradation. He advocates a stateless society in which people live in decentralized communities, governing themselves in small, face-to-face democracies.[37]

Another voice advocating radical political change to protect the environment is Barry Commoner's. He reasons that the state of the environment is determined by the production technologies used by manufacturing, agriculture, and transportation. As long as technology decisions are in the hands of private corporations, he says, efforts to improve environmental quality will have little effect. The choice of technologies for all potentially damaging industries should be a "social responsibility." If it were, the first consideration would be the state of the environment, not the economic viability of the industry.[38]

The new, awkwardly fitting, ideas added to environmentalism have come primarily from the grassroots toxics groups. Still epitomized by the Love Canal Homeowners Association but now found throughout the country, grassroots groups ignore the initial environmentalist concerns such as wilderness and endangered species. In their view, the environment does not need to be protected from humans; humans need to be protected from the environment. Moreover, the environment they talk about is not far away in some vacationland or foreign country, but in their own neighborhoods—something they experience every day. They have stretched environmentalism to include the noise and stench from corporate hog farming and the unemployment rates and decayed housing that plague life in inner cities. Augmenting the anthropocentrist focus on human beings, grassroots activists contend that the environmental crisis is not equally shared. In the late 1980s they began using the term environmental justice to describe their goal, and they have given wide publicity to studies showing that poor people and people of color are more likely to live near hazardous waste facilities than are other people. Grassroots groups add to environmentalism the concepts of fairness and justice to humans.[39]

Scholarly critiques of environmentalist thought fall into two groups. One consists of ecologists who dispute a central environmentalist idea: that nature free from human interference achieves a state of perfect balance. These ecologists, prominent among them Daniel Botkin and Michael Barbour, point to new ecological studies that reveal not order, constancy, and stability in nature but continual change without a predictable pattern. In every place, they say, the number of any given species at any particular time could be high or low, and the numbers do not oscillate in equilibrium.[40] Such studies rob environmentalism of its assumption that a perfect state of nature exists. They thus undercut the environmentalist principle that humans must not interfere with nature, for if there is no pattern, how could there be interference?

The other group of scholars makes a similar critique, but from the perspective of the humanities and social sciences. They argue that "nature" is a social construction and thus cannot objectively be distinguished from non-nature. In any culture, they say, what gets recognized as natural depends on who is doing the recognizing and when and for what purpose the recognizing occurs. William Cronon, the editor of a collection of essays elaborating on this point, says that "people pour into [the word nature] all their most personal and culturally specific values; the essence of who they think they are, how and where they should live, what they believe to be good and beautiful, why people should act in certain ways."[41]

Neither ecologists like Botkin and Barbour nor constructivists like Cronon oppose environmentalism. Botkin writes:

> The task that I am encouraging the reader to join in... acknowledges the great destructive powers of human civilization but is optimistic that we may begin to choose as a prudent person would in our dealings with nature.... [The task is] consistent with the land ethic of Aldo Leopold: "Conservation is a state of harmony between men and land." We have not abandoned that belief or Leopold's ethic, but have redefined "harmony."[42]

And Cronon says that his analysis comes from within the environmental movement. "Indeed," he writes, speaking for the contributors to his book, "it is precisely because we sympathize so strongly with the environmentalist agenda—with the task of rethinking and reconstructing human relationships with the natural world to make them just and accountable—that we believe those questions must be confronted."[43]

By the same token, anthropocentrists say that they support environmentalism's ethical and ecological principles as firmly as do ecocentrists. In Murray Bookchin's words:

> I share a good deal of the ecological state of mind of my conservation friends.... Our society has got to learn to live in peace with the planet, with the rest of the biosphere. We are in complete agreement on this fundamental point. We now live under the constant threat that the world of life will be irrevocably undermined by a society gone mad in its need to grow—replacing the organic by the inorganic, soil by concrete, forest by barren earth, and the diversity of life-forms by simplified ecosystems.[44]

And the grassroots movement, for all its emphasis on the environment as a source of harm instead of a fragile entity needing our protection, is not opposed to environmentalism. A good piece of evidence is the document drawn up in 1991 at the First National People of Color Environmental Leadership Summit. The Summit brought 600 grassroots activists from all over the country to Washington, D.C., for five days. Their task was to develop a collective response to the unequal distribution of hazardous waste facilities. The most formal outcome was a now widely circulated list of seventeen "Principles of Environmental Justice." Principle number one reads: "Environmental Justice affirms the sacredness of Mother Earth, ecological unity and the interdependence of all species, and the right to be free from ecological destruction."[45]

Support for Environmentalism

I have been arguing that environmentalism was a new phenomenon in the second half of the twentieth century. Developed and promoted by a variety of social critics, it introduced into industrial society the idea that all of nature is endangered. Its supporters have disagreed about why the environment is endangered, what constitutes the environment, and how nature works. But even in their disagreements, they continue to promote environmentalism's basic message. The question now is how successfully they have promoted it. I don't mean, "How many natural resources have been protected, and how much pollution has been reduced?" Those are, of course, the ultimate questions, but the question I am asking here is, "How many ordinary citizens have adopted environmentalist principles?" One way to find out is to look at national polling data. These suggest that the number is quite high.

All the major polls began asking questions about the environment in the 1970s. At no time, either then or now, have people rated the environment as the most important public problem, but the percentage of respondents concerned about environmental quality has increased considerably since the first polls. Today, a large majority seems to accept the environmentalist principle that the environment is endangered. (There are, however, interesting differences between men and women and between blacks and whites.[46]) For example, polling data suggest that well over two-thirds of the general population now think the government's spending on the environment is insufficient. Asked in 1990 whether the government was spending too little, about right, or too much on the environment, 71 percent of respondents said "too little." This was a big increase from 1980, when only 49 percent had said so. Somewhat fewer people—only 62 percent—thought there was not enough government regulation of the environment in 1990, but this was still a majority, and it was a jump from 1982, when only 35 percent wanted more environmental regulation.

An even larger percentage of people say they favor environmental protection even if it costs a lot. In a 1990 poll, 74 percent of respondents agreed with the statement "Protecting the environment is so important that requirements and standards cannot be too high, and continuing environmental improvements must be made regardless of cost." In 1981, when the same statement was posed, only 41 percent had agreed. Getting more specific, another survey posed a choice between sacrificing environmental quality for economic growth or sacrificing economic growth for environmental quality. In 1990, 64 percent of respondents chose environmental quality over economic growth. Nine years earlier only 41 percent of respondents had made that choice.[47]

In addition to questions about environmental policies, one poll (Gallup) has twice asked, "Do you consider yourself to be an environmentalist, or not?" In 1991, a remarkable 78 percent of people polled said they did. The percentage fell later: in 1995 only 63 percent said so. Yet even the lower figure is impressive. In the mid-1960s environmentalism did not even exist. Thirty years later, over half the people in this country identified with it.

These polls do not tell us, however, what people mean when they say they are environmentalists. We know they believe the environment is endangered and that we must change our ways in order to save it. But do they accept the other two environmentalist principles? That is, do they believe that people should not interfere in the balance of nature and that nature is intrinsically valuable? For answers to this question, we can turn to two surveys. Both indicate that the answer to the question is yes. The first survey was administered by Lester Milbrath in 1980 and again in 1982. Of the 96 questionnaire items, five were specifically about what Milbrath called the "environmental perspective" (a group of statements garnered from interviews with members of environmental organizations). Milbrath presented statements based on this perspective to seven groups of people (labor leaders, appointed officials, elected officials, business leaders, environmentalists, media gatekeepers, and the general public). I list the 1982 responses to these five questions from the general public.[48]

Statement	Percent rejecting	Percent accepting
Humans must live in harmony with nature in order to survive.	8	87
Mankind is severely abusing the environment.	17	76
A society should save its resources to benefit future generations rather than using them for the present generation.	14	73
I cherish nature and preserve it as one of the most precious things in life.	14	76
A country should encourage people to adapt to their natural environment rather than remake it to suit their needs.	15	71

Note: Persons taking a neutral position on these questions are not reported in the table; hence, the percentages will not add to 100.

These are startlingly high agreement levels. The numbers suggest that some three-quarters of the general population had adopted environmentalist values by 1982. If we had data from a similar pre-environmentalist survey showing much less agreement with these values, we could be sure that assimilation of environmentalist values had risen sharply over the years. Possibly most people in the mid-1960s would have agreed that we should live in harmony with nature and consider it pre-

cious and that we should adapt to the natural environment and save resources. Even if they had not thought much about such things before,
they may have thought these were nice goals. Probably fewer people
would have agreed with the idea that we were severely abusing the environment. And that statement is much more critical, in both senses of the
word. Instead of implying simple respect for nature, it implies an embrace of environmentalism. We need more such statements in opinion
polls before we can conclude that the general public now embraces environmentalist principles.

Fortunately, such statements are found in a survey done by Willett
Kempton, James S. Boster, and Jennifer A. Hartley. The survey was administered between 1989 and 1991 to five groups of people: (1) members of Earth First! in Vermont and Wisconsin (representing radical environmentalists), (2) members of the Sierra Club in Southern California
(representing moderate environmentalists), (3) the "lay public" in
northern and southern California, (4) managers of dry-cleaning shops
in Los Angeles (whose businesses were threatened by new air pollution
regulations), and (5) laid-off sawmill workers in Oregon (whose layoff
may have been due to environmentalist public policies). This 149-item
survey covered a somewhat wider variety of topics than the Milbrath
survey, and it included thirty-seven statements specifically about environmental values. Importantly, for all but five of the statements, the majority of the general public, the dry cleaners, and the sawmill workers es-
poused the ethical and ecological principles that environmentalists
promote. In the authors' words, the study's "surprising (and encouraging) news is that despite some differences when comparing opposite
extremes, there is a remarkably strong consensus across this wide spectrum on a core set of environmental values."[49]

Most of the people queried thought that nature has intrinsic value and
should be preserved for its own sake. They agreed with statements that
used the terms *justice, obligation,* and *spiritual value,* in relation to nature
(Table 1, page 56). Another group of statements in the survey reflect the
ecological notion that nature is interrelated and that interference is
likely to be dangerous. Here, too, respondents across the spectrum expressed strong agreement (Table 2, page 57). When the statement was
reversed, suggesting that it is all right for humans to use nature for their
own ends, only a minority agreed (Table 3, page 58).

Kempton and his colleagues have data from a very small sample of
the population—only 142 respondents—but the percentage of the

Table 1.

No.	Statement	Earth First! (%)	Sierra Club (%)	Public (%)	Dry Cleaners (%)	Sawmill Workers (%)
16	Justice is not just for human beings, we need to be as fair to plants and animals as we are toward people.	97	85	90	83	63
27	We have a moral duty to leave the earth in as good or better shape than we found it.	100	100	100	97	96
51	Our obligation to preserve nature isn't just a responsibility to other people but to the environment itself.	97	100	87	90	82
124	Species of plants and animals have intrinsic aesthetic and spiritual value even if they are not of any use to humans.	100	96	83	87	70

Table 2.

No.	Statement	Earth First! (%)	Sierra Club (%)	Public (%)	Dry Cleaners (%)	Sawmill Workers (%)
57	Global climate change would disturb the whole chain of life.	100	85	93	90	82
77	Humans should recognize they are part of nature and shouldn't try to control or manipulate it.	97	74	72	57	69
105	Nature has complex interdependencies. Any human meddling will cause a chain reaction with unanticipated effects.	97	89	77	76	63

Table 3.

No.	Statement	Earth First! (%)	Sierra Club (%)	Public (%)	Dry Cleaners (%)	Sawmill Workers (%)
29	The environment may have been abused, but it has tremendous recuperative powers. The radical measures being taken to protect the environment are not necessary and will cause too much economic harm.	0	7	23	17	33
132	We shouldn't be too worried about environmental damage. Technology is developing so fast that, in the future, people will be able to repair most of the environmental damage that has been done.	0	4	10	13	15

sample that agreed with environmentalist values is remarkably high. There was overwhelming agreement with the statements whose language and concepts were forthrightly environmentalist. (The phrases come right out of writings by Carson, Leopold, and today's environmental organizations.) This survey, taken together with the much larger Milbrath survey (which in 1982 had 695 respondents in the U.S. sample alone) underscores the conclusion reached by two Gallup analysts: "The most obvious achievement of the environmental movement has been the development of a national consensus that acknowledges the seriousness of environmental problems."[50]

There are other indications of environmentalists' success. One is what Robert Booth Fowler calls the greening of Protestant thought. Fowler says that a vibrant ecotheology, which has been developing in Protestant religions since the late 1960s, integrates the traditional Protestant commitment to community with environmentalist visions of ecological harmony and an interdependent nature.[51] Another indicator is the spread of environmental education in the public school system and the popularity of environmental studies in colleges and universities. As C. A. Bowers points out, environmentalists have focused on formal education as a means to transform cultural assumptions about nature.[52] This education is bolstered by the EPA's Office of Environmental Education, which has given out approximately $16 million in grants since 1992.[53] A third indicator of environmentalists' success is the structure of the environmental laws passed since 1970, which threaten polluters with fines and jail terms. Such laws, as David Spence reminds us, reflect the idea that pollution is immoral, not, as some scholars and economists argue, simply the natural (but lamentable) consequence of market forces.[54] Yet another indicator is the growth of ecotourism. According to one estimate, ecotourism will be the largest industry in the world by 2000, in terms of employment and trade. It caters to the surge in environmental consciousness, offering tourists views of nature unsullied by modern development.[55] Finally, there is the replication of environmentalist principles in popular culture. The concept that nature is endangered, so oft repeated in television programs and movies—especially those directed to children—has become common fare.[56] The idea that nature is pure and good is now a central concept for an entire business sector. As Jennifer Price says, probably every mall in America has some store like the Nature Company, devoted entirely to products that are "images of nature, pieces of nature, and tools for going out into nature."[57]

Over the past thirty years or so, environmentalists have developed and promoted a new view of nature. They have taken the scientific principle that all of nature is interconnected and the ethical principle that all of nature is precious and have linked them to the new political principle that all of nature is endangered so we must act now to save it. Although these environmentalist ideas are being constantly adapted and contestated from inside the environmental movement and flatly opposed by at least some people outside the movement, a remarkably large number of Americans embraces them. Environmentalism is no longer a collection of ideas about nature that people have to defend against a culturally dominant opposition. Instead, for larger and larger numbers of people, environmentalism has become a fairly coherent worldview they simply take for granted. In saying so, I follow several other scholars. Among them are Kempton and his colleagues, who conclude their book by asserting that environmentalism is now well integrated into American core values, and Robert Paehlke, who says that environmentalism is poised to be as influential a body of thought as liberalism and socialism.[58]

Neither the public opinion surveys nor the other indicators of environmentalists' success reveal who or what the public blames for environmental degradation or who or what the public thinks must change in order to restore environmental integrity. The actors in the Milbrath survey are "humans," "mankind," "society," and "the country." The survey by Kempton and his collaborators asks about "our obligation" and "our duty"; it points to what "we need" and "we have." This language fails to distinguish between actions that governments and industries should take and actions that individual citizens should take. It does not, in other words, tell us how many of the respondents agree with the environmentalists who argue that only a change in the basic political economy will protect the environment and how many agree with the environmentalists who argue that change on the individual level will be sufficient. Despite this vagueness in the data, the surveys do indicate that most Americans have strong pro-environmentalist sentiments.

If some sort of environmentalism is now or is about to become part of American core values, we should expect these new principles to affect a variety of contemporary institutions. And indeed, religion, education, government, tourism, and popular culture all now reflect environmental principles. But we should also look for its influence on science. Environmentalism's most radical influence on science would be to make illegitimate the reductionism on which scientific investigations depend. Although nothing of the sort seems to be happening, the spread of environmentalism has quite obviously attracted more scientists to ecological research. Less noticed is environmentalism's effect on the practice of environmental epidemiology. I will argue in the next chapter that this field, although still heavily influenced by pre-environmentalist ideas, now shows signs of change that would bring it into line with the new ways of thinking about nature. As this change occurs, scientists will more easily be able to correlate a community's exposure to pollution with health problems.

4 Environmentalist Science

The suggestion at the end of the last chapter, that environmentalism will affect science, rests on the idea that science is socially constructed. That idea, in turn, is usually traced to the publication, in 1962 and again in 1970, of Thomas Kuhn's *The Structure of Scientific Revolutions*. In this enormously influential book, Kuhn argues that scientific communities are governed by "paradigms," or shared views of the world, which are themselves not the objects of scientific study but the assumptions from which each scientific discipline begins.[1] These paradigms are indispensable, for without them researchers would not know what kinds of questions are appropriate for investigation, what observations are pertinent, what methods are legitimate, and what answers are acceptable. At the same time, says Kuhn, paradigms act as blinders, limiting scientists' ability to observe the world around them. Phenomena "that will not fit the box are often not seen at all."[2]

Kuhn says that when the number of phenomena outside the box grows to proportions that can no longer be ignored, science goes through a "revolution." Scientists throw over the old paradigm and replace it with a new one. The new one makes them see the world differently.

> Led by a new paradigm, scientists adopt new instruments and look in new places. Even more important, during revolutions scientists see new and different things when looking with familiar instruments in places they have looked before.[3]

Kuhn does not evaluate paradigms. To him new ones are not necessarily preferable to old ones. He just wants to show that paradigms are inevitable and thus that no clear line can entirely separate science from culture, facts from values, objective from subjective reasoning. Not all the philosophers and historians of science inspired by Kuhn take such a neutral position. Many are social critics. They argue that some paradigms have generated scientific questions, methodologies, and findings that legitimate social inequalities. These scholars differ from Kuhn in another respect, too. They say that the paradigms underlying scientific research are not only the "beliefs, values, techniques, and so on shared by members of a given [scientific] community,"[4] as Kuhn understood them, but also the beliefs and values of the general society. As long as those beliefs and values are uncontested, few people notice their effects on science. But during periods of social upheaval, when new social values challenge old ones, culture's effect on science is more visible, especially to advocates of the new values. Consider, for example, the arguments by feminists about patriarchal values.

Evelyn Fox Keller says that for years most scientists ignored the work of geneticist Barbara McClintock because it derived from a logic utterly at odds with the masculinist view of reality dominating genetics. Studying the process by which genetic information is transferred in cell division, McClintock saw a process of complex interaction wherein DNA can move around from one chromosomal site to another in response to the changing needs of the organism. McClintock's discovery flew in the face of James Watson and Francis Crick's announcement that genetic information, not subject to modification, flows downward from a central actor to subordinate agents. It was this concept of a "master molecule," says Keller, that made immediate sense to most scientists. Fitting with their assumption that the world is ordered hierarchically, and that those at the bottom should take direction from those at the top, it dominated genetics for a very long time.[5]

McClintock's ideas about the transposition of genetic elements are now firmly established within genetics, but Keller argues that science as a whole is still so infused with patriarchy that it sanctions unjust prerogatives.[6] Donna Haraway agrees. "The degree to which the principle of domination is deeply embedded in our natural sciences," she says, "must not be underestimated."[7] In her analysis of animal sociology, Haraway describes an influential study of monkeys that sought to understand how social order is created and maintained. The investigator of that study started with the unexamined assumption that societies are like single organisms in that they have only one head. So he identified a dominant male in several groups of monkeys. Then he removed that monkey from each group and observed that the monkeys competed until a new male asserted control and harmony was restored. The investigation, says Haraway, inaccurately presumed that social order depends on dominance and that competition is the precondition of cooperation. She argues that a study of the same monkeys focusing on the females instead of on the males would have seen organization as "long-term social cooperation rather than short-term spectacular aggression, flexible process rather than strict structure, and so on."[8]

In a similar vein, Emily Martin shows how gender stereotypes affect reproductive biologists' observations, as well as bolster the stereotypes. Scientific journals and textbooks, she argues, describe the fertilization process in terms that assign the egg and the sperm traditional male and female social roles. The egg sits around passively waiting for the industrious sperm to swim up to it and give its existence meaning. She gives a striking example from a 1984 textbook whose authors liken the egg to Sleeping Beauty: "a dormant bride awaiting her mate's magic kiss, which instills the spirit that brings her to life." Sperm, by contrast, have a "mission," which is to "move through the female genital tract in quest of the ovum."[9]

Later investigators found that sperm are weak swimmers and that rather than invading an egg, they hitch themselves onto its surface and are gradually sucked in—a process aided by a digestive enzyme in the sperm and an adhesive coating on both egg and sperm. Despite this finding, so powerful are gender stereotypes that for a long time even "the researchers who made the discovery continued to write papers and abstracts as if the sperm were the active party who attacks, binds, penetrates, and enters the egg."[10]

Whereas these feminists show how unexamined cultural assumptions can blind scientists to certain phenomena, other social critics show how unexamined assumptions affect the questions scientists set out to answer in the first place. For example, in their critique of U.S. government vital statistics Nancy Krieger and Elizabeth Fee argue that, although variations among people are greater within races than among races (pointing out that we all share about 95 percent of our genetic heritage), a deeply held belief in racial differences makes it seem logical to categorize morbidity and mortality data according to race.[11] With such categorization, government statisticians are, in effect, asking how biological difference accounts for inequalities in health. They take for granted that difference does so. Krieger and Fee show that statisticians and epidemiologists who start with the assumption of biological *similarities* ask not about the effects of race on health but about the effects of racism, a question that lends itself to more-effective disease prevention policies.

Similarly, Stephen Jay Gould argues that Western culture's linearity—our belief in progress and our "propensity for ordering complex variation on a gradual ascending scale"—has prompted scientists to ask how people can most accurately be ranked. In the nineteenth century, scientists measured skulls, an exercise that showed that some whole groups of people, notably white males, were smarter (and thus more deserving) than other groups. In the twentieth century, they measured "intelligence quotients" with the same intent and result. What Gould objects to is not just the reinforcement of prejudice and the naturalization of inequalities. It is the whole project of reducing a person's life to a single number. This is a theory of limits, he says. Were our culture less concerned with fixing "related things into a progressive chain of being,"[12] scientists would more likely pose questions about human possibilities.

But in Gould's view, unexamined cultural assumptions do not hold all scientists captive. In the first place, some scientists do ask questions and propose answers incongruent with mainstream ideology. Gould's work itself is an example. So is the work of Barbara McClintock and the other scientists I discussed above. In the second place, cultures change. New values shove old ones aside. Events and situations that most people once took for granted come to be seen as unjust. It is the effect such cultural changes have on science that I explore in this chapter. My exploration throws a different light on social constructivism. Many authors' essays focus on negative aspects of the culture-science link. They show how scientists unwittingly design studies that both reflect and support inegalitarian values. I am interested in positive aspects of the culture-science link. What scientific investigations reflect egalitarian values? To answer the question, I look at changes occurring today in environmental epidemiology.

Signs of Change

As Chapter Three shows, environmentalists have worked hard to generate and promote a novel view of nature. They argue that instead of lacking intrinsic value, nature has its own integrity and thus should be revered; that instead of being divisible into discrete parts, nature is intricately interconnected and thus best understood as an organic whole;

and that instead of being tough and resilient, nature is highly vulnerable to harm from human technology and thus endangered. We have seen that the general public appears to have embraced these previously eccentric ideas. They have also had an impact, however, on environmental health scientists. Evidence for the impact comes from new developments in risk assessment, the protocol I describe in Chapter Two, which the EPA uses to determine whether a substance is a public health hazard.

Since the mid-1980s, when risk assessment was adopted by the federal government, environmentalists have lodged at least five complaints against it. First, they say, risk assessment concentrates on cancer instead of focusing on the whole range of diseases that can result from exposure to pollution. Second, it presupposes that people are all alike in susceptibility instead of attending to their biological and social diversity. Third, it takes clinical illness as the expression of harm instead of noting that harm manifests itself in many other ways. Fourth, it presumes that chemicals behave independently instead of taking into consideration synergistic interactions among them. And fifth, it demands an extremely high standard of proof before it will conclude that exposure to pollution is harmful.[13]

In sum, the critics charge that risk assessment reflects a pre-environmentalist view of nature. Despite the fact that the risk assessment protocol was developed in response to worries that synthetic chemicals are health hazards, the protocol carries with it the very reductionism that environmentalism opposes. Its concentration on a single disease, its compression of all of humanity into a single person, its narrow view of illness, and its atomistic concept of chemicals all contrast sharply with the wholism environmentalists promote. Furthermore, risk assessment's high standard of proof clashes with the environmentalist principle that human interference in natural processes is probably dangerous. What the critics tacitly call for is an *environmentalist* epidemiology, one that sees the world in terms of a broad network of intricate interconnections and one that recognizes that the air, water, and soil are, in many parts of the world, probably dangerously polluted. Such a science, they imply, would be more in keeping with reality and therefore a better instrument for discovering the health problems caused by exposure to toxic substances.

Calling for a new kind of epidemiology is hardly new. The field of study has experienced several internal reformations since it became a science in the early nineteenth century—each reformation consistent with a new theory of disease causality, each one fought over by competing groups of scientists, and each one reflecting larger social changes.[14] Whether epidemiology will change again in response to environmentalism cannot be known today, when environmentalist ideas are still so new to industrial society. But it is possible to discern new preoccupations among scientists that may signal the beginning of a shift to an environmentalist study of disease, one more likely to demonstrate that exposure to synthetic chemicals endangers public health.

Beyond Cancer

One sign of change is the gathering interest in outcomes of exposure other than cancer. Although researchers have correlated environmental pollutants with many kinds of adverse health conditions, when the Environmental Protection Agency evaluates the scientific information on the hazardous properties of environmental pollutants, it concentrates on cancer data. The focus on cancer fits well with early environmentalism. In *Silent Spring*, Rachel Carson barely mentioned other diseases; the whole book seemed to say that synthetic chemicals cause only cancer. Even to this day, "toxic chemical" is in both the popular and scientific imagination largely synonymous with "carcinogen." But the coupling has big drawbacks for environmentalism. It means that when suspect chemicals are found not to cause cancer, the rationale for them to be called toxic is shaken. It also means that investigators are less likely to look for, and thus less likely to find, links between exposure to pollution and other health problems.

In recent years, however, some scientists have been looking for, and finding, a connection between environmental pollution and other outcomes in wildlife and in humans. Those receiving the most attention are impaired sexual development (such as decreased sperm counts and undescended testicles), reproductive problems (such as infertility, birth defects, and endometriosis), and cognitive dysfunctions (such as low IQ scores, learning disabilities, and behavioral immaturity). Although for the most part the data on wildlife are stronger than the data on humans, the tradition in environmental health sciences of using animals as proxies for humans gives the data high value. The research on these maladies gained coherence when the chemicals linked to them were grouped together under a new term: endocrine disruptors. Suddenly there is a new category of ailments related to environmental pollution. Instead of just cancers plus an unwieldy assortment of other possible outcomes of exposure, there are now two firm classifications: cancers and hormone-related conditions. Each kind of malady is dreadful, but hormone-related conditions are especially frightening because they concern an entire, highly complex, physiological system. In the words of one environmentalist, they affect "the very characteristics that make us human."[15]

By the end of 1997, nearly three hundred peer-reviewed studies on endocrine disrupters had been published. Fifty-one endocrine-disrupting substances had been identified—including DDT, kepone, lindane, some PCB cogeners, several dioxins, cadmium, lead, mercury, alkyl phenols, and diethylstilbestrol (DES). And the EPA had put endocrine disrupters among its top five research issues.[16]

The person most acclaimed for identifying this new category of disease is Theo Colborn, an environmental endocrine researcher at the World Wildlife Fund, a convener of the 1991 Wingspread Conference, which first brought together scientists working on synthetic hormones, and the principle author of *Our Stolen Future*, described by Vice President Al Gore in an introduction (and by several reviewers) as the sequel to *Silent Spring*. At the end of the book, Colborn and her colleagues advocate large changes in industrial society, saying we must phase out "hormone-disrupting chemicals [and] slow down the larger experiment with synthetic chemicals,... curtailing the introduction of thousands of new synthetic chemicals each year [and] reducing the use of pesticides as much as possible."[17] These are familiar words coming from environmentalists, and possibly the endocrine-disrupter research will lend them new urgency. But the more immediate impact of the research may be on what Colborn and her colleagues call the cancer paradigm:

> If this book [*Our Stolen Future*] contains a single prescriptive message, it is this: we must move beyond the cancer paradigm.... This is not simply an argument for broadening our horizons to recognize additional risks. We need to bring new concepts to our consideration of toxic chemicals. The assumptions about toxicity and disease that have framed our thinking for the past three decades are inappropriate and act as obstacles to understanding a different kind of damage.[18]

One obstacle created by the cancer paradigm, they argue, is the assumption that dose and response are always positively correlated. Relying on the cancer paradigm, environmental toxicologists and epidemiologists assumed that high doses are more dangerous than low doses. But endocrine disrupters do not work like carcinogens. The physiological response to them may increase with the dose for a while and then start to diminish.[19] So if scientists used endocrine disrupters instead of carcinogens as a model for predicting the human health effects of exposure to pollutants, they might come up with quite different risk assessments. People exposed to low doses could be at greater risk than people exposed to high doses. One result of this new model could be more persistent epidemiologists. They would have new reason to suspect a community exposed to low levels of environmental pollution had been harmed and thus become more dogged in their attempts to find evidence of it.

Another obstacle is the assumption that individuals directly exposed to pollution are the most appropriate focus of study. The research on cancer leads investigators to think of environmental pollutants as poisons and to assume that pollutants kill cells or attack DNA. But endocrine disrupters do not resemble poisons. Instead they are more like CIA operatives. They are "thugs on the biological information highways.... They jam signals. They scramble messages. They sow disinformation."[20] And because the messages they scramble are hormone messages, these pollutants may affect not the individual directly exposed to them but the next generation. The best-known example is the case of DES daughters; these women, whose mothers took the synthetic hormone diethylstilbestrol when they were pregnant, developed reproductive tract deformities after puberty. Applying this model to environmental exposures, Colborn and her colleagues suggest that after the 1976 chemical plant explosion in Seveso, Italy, epidemiologists may have investigated the wrong population or the right population at the wrong time. Epidemiologists asked whether cancer rates had gone up among the victims and whether there were obvious birth defects. Finding none, they announced that the explosion had not harmed human health. But investigators using endocrine disrupters as a model, say Colborn and her colleagues, would have looked for "damage invisible at birth, such as delayed effects on the endocrine, immune, and nervous systems."[21] Whether or not new investigations will find such effects, these are the kinds of issues the model prompts researchers to pursue.

Special Groups

A second sign of change toward a less reductionist and more environmentalist science is the new attention to distinctive population groups. Until very recently, risk assessment as well as environmental epidemiology operated under what Robert Verchick calls a "one size fits all" theory.[22] The average person was taken to be a white, middle-class adult, and environmental health studies with this narrow focus were assumed to reveal everything science needed to know about the public's vulnerability to environmental toxins.[23] Now, however, two distinctive groups have been carved out of "the public" and identified as distinctive. One is children. The other is racial minorities and poor people. Both groups are held to be especially susceptible to pollution—children because of their biological characteristics, racial minorities and poor people because of their location at the bottom of the social hierarchy. As a result of recognizing these differences, any community's claim that pollution has affected their health may become easier to demonstrate.

The first big rush of publicity singling out children as especially vulnerable to environmental toxins came in February 1989 when *60 Minutes* ran an emotional story about Alar residues on apples. As I describe in more detail in the next chapter, the story, reporting on a study designed by scientists at the Natural Resources Defense Council (NRDC), said that, because children ingest more food in relation to their body weight than adults, they get relatively more pesticide exposure.[24] Four years later, the National Research Council finished its own investigation on children and pesticides. The study, which was headed by Philip Landrigan, a long-time proponent of strong environmental policies, corroborated the NRDC's points about children's sensitivity and called for stricter controls on pesticides.[25]

Congress responded to the National Research Council's recommendations in 1996 by passing the Food Quality Protection Act, which requires the EPA to tighten its exposure standards for pesticides enough to ensure a tenfold margin of safety. Later that year President Bill Clinton announced that the EPA would use children's health to guide all environmental health regulations.[26] Carol Browner, EPA administrator, quickly followed up with a proposal for new Clean Air Act regulations, and in the ensuing controversy she and other supporters of tighter standards regularly appealed to the special needs of children.[27] In the meantime, the EPA established a new center for children's health, headed by Philip Landrigan.

The Department of Health and Human Services has joined the campaign. Its National Institute for Environmental Health Studies (NIEHS; located in the National Institutes of Health) has made children's environmental health a major focus. Together with a citizens' environmental

group, the Children's Environmental Health Network, it organized conferences in 1994 and 1997 on the topic and subsequently published the
proceedings in the NIEHS journal *Environmental Health Perspectives*. The
journal's editors specifically encourage submissions on children's environmental health.[28]

The full implications of identifying children as especially vulnerable
are clear if you think about the Agency for Toxic Substances and Disease
Registry (ATSDR) and the EPA. The ATSDR (located in the U.S. Public
Health Service) does health assessments at Superfund sites. When it de-
termines that "human exposure to dangerous levels of hazardous substances has occurred, is occurring, or is likely to occur in the short
term," the EPA is required to act.[29] But what are dangerous levels? At the
time this policy was adopted, the EPA was using studies on white middle-
class adults to determine dangerous levels of pollution. Now, if children's health is guiding all regulations, dangerous levels will be different. Whatever is dangerous to children will be what is dangerous to
everybody. Of course, the fact that investigators find dangerous levels of
hazardous substances in a community is not enough to conclude that
living there makes people sick. The ATSDR also considers whether and
to what extent people are actually exposed to the substances. But the
changed definition of dangerous levels means that some people who
used to live in certified "safe" communities may now suddenly, without
moving, live in certified "dangerous" communities.

A similar phenomena has occurred by defining minorities and poor
people as especially vulnerable to environmental pollution. Attention to
race and poverty and the environment was not initially covered in the
national media as was the story about children and the environment,
nor was it prompted by investigations by environmentalist scientists. Instead, it began with a group of ordinary people, most of them African
Americans, who were trying to keep PCB-laden soil from being dumped
in their neighborhood. During a public demonstration, the police arrested a U.S Congressman, and when the enraged Congressman re-
turned to Washington, he asked the U.S General Accounting Office to
investigate the link between race and the location of hazardous waste
dumps. The resulting document (published in 1983) showed that three
out of four landfills in the Southeast were in poor and African American
neighborhoods. Four years later, the United Church of Christ's Commission on Racial Justice released the results of a larger investigation. This
one looked at all 415 operating commercial hazardous waste landfills in

the United States, as well at as all 18,164 closed or abandoned hazardous waste sites. It concluded that in the nation as a whole, communities with the largest number of hazardous waste facilities have a disproportionate percentage of racial and ethnic minorities and that race is a more significant indicator of the location of these hazardous waste facilities than is socioeconomic status.[30] At least fifteen other studies have come to similar conclusions, some focusing on race and some on poverty.[31]

Although a number of scholars have criticized the methodology used in the major studies on race and the environment,[32] the EPA responded to the studies by creating, in 1992, an Office of Environmental Equity. Four years later, President Clinton announced an executive order requiring all federal agencies to make environmental justice part of their mission, and the Council on Environmental Quality (CEQ) issued a "Guidance for Considering Environmental Justice Under the National Environmental Policy Act." Both the EPA and the White House are vague about what environmental justice actions agency personnel are supposed to take. But the CEQ document says that, before the EPA issues a permit to a polluting industry, it must consider the ways that cultural, occupational, historical, and economic factors could intensify the pollution's effect on the community.[33] In essence, the EPA must adopt environmentalism's complex view of the world, recognizing interlinkages and multiple causations.

The requirement proposes a significant change in the way scientists study the relationship between public health and environmental pollution. They now have to consider the possibility that the same toxic chemical could have worse health effects in poor communities than in wealthy ones. Such a reevaluation of pollution occurred in 1997 in two predominately African American communities: one in Michigan, the other in Louisiana. In Michigan, residents managed to keep a local waste incinerator from burning contaminated demolition wood by arguing that they had already been dumped on by so many other nearby sources of hazardous waste that their bodies could not handle any more toxins. They were, in a sense, already full up, and risk assessments that failed to take their toxic overload into consideration were too low.[34] Similarly, in Louisiana, residents foiled the owner of a uranium-enrichment plant by arguing that the plant would expose them to more pollution than had been estimated, because, being poor, they relied more than most people on food from their gardens and on hunting and fishing.[35]

So, as has the new attention on children, the new focus on race and class may have made risky what was once considered safe. With the requirement to take into account an exposed group's entire social situation, a "dangerous level" of exposure is no longer simply that which puts middle-class whites at risk. The health of minorities and poor people might be endangered by much lower levels. Both changes—the identification of children as more physiologically sensitive than adults and the identification of minorities and poor people as probably *already* living in more-polluted neighborhoods than the "average" person—make it easier to demonstrate that pollution causes disease.

Chemical Mixtures

A third sign of change toward a more environmentalist epidemiology is the gathering interest in chemical mixtures. Risk assessment assumes that each chemical in the environment has its own inherent properties. Some chemicals are very toxic; some are mildly toxic; some are benign. Thus, even if people are exposed to a great many chemicals at once—a "toxic soup" in popular imagery—if each individual component of the soup is benign, no one's health is at risk.

This inherently reductionistic assumption is challenged by research showing that certain chemicals that are innocuous individually become toxic when mixed together.[36] The research has obvious implications for environmental epidemiology. If investigators assume that toxic properties are only additive, when in fact they are synergistic, risks at some sites could be seriously underestimated. Thinking that residents' health problems simply could not be due to environmental exposures, epidemiologists could erroneously attribute any excess morbidity or mortality to other causes or to chance.

Steve Wing and his colleagues argue that investigators at Three Mile Island (TMI) made exactly that error. The issue there was radiation, not chemical mixtures, but the principle is the same. In a study of cancer rates at TMI after the 1979 accident, one group of epidemiologists found elevated rates of several cancers. But the exposure data they were working with showed that radiation doses were too low to produce those effects, so the researchers concluded that cancers were unrelated to the accident.[37] In their study, Wing and his colleagues had data showing that radiation doses in some areas *were* high enough to produce cancer. Thus they were able to attribute elevated rates to the accident.[38] In essence, the first study found TMI safe, and the second found it hazardous. The major difference between the two was their initial assumptions about the toxicity of the pollutant the residents were exposed to.

The research on mixtures received an apparently big boost in 1996 when a group of investigators at Tulane University, experimenting on yeast cells, found that combinations of some estrogen-disrupting chemicals are a thousand times more toxic than any of the chemicals alone.[39] The finding was published in *Science* and was widely reported in the popular press. *Science* itself hailed the research. An accompanying editorial linked the Tulane findings to the new field of endocrine disorder and praised the Tulane group for providing evidence that the levels of estrogen disrupters in the environment are high enough to harm humans.[40] A year later, however, in an act unusual for science, the Tulane team withdrew the paper when investigators at other universities were unable to replicate their findings.[41] For environmentalists, hoping for strong evidence that synthetic chemicals harm human health even at low levels, the Tulane story is a setback. But many environmental health scientists are still intensely interested in synergistic chemical reactions. The editors of *Environmental Health Perspectives* urge readers not to let the problems with yeast studies distract them "from the larger issues." Although effective research strategies still need to be designed, they say, it is clear from earlier work "with PCBs and several pesticide formulations that synergy and antagonism may occur in circumstances of multiple chemical exposures."[42] A month later the same journal ran an editorial by an EPA scientist discussing some of the problems in understanding the effects of chemical mixtures. In a conclusion full of environmentalist imagery, he said:

> There clearly is a need to expand our thinking about this problem area.... Although many/most of these chemicals may function as imperfect hormones with relatively low potencies, we have not begun to understand what the potential adverse effects are of being exposed continuously to complex mixtures of chemicals with varying abilities to affect multiple signaling pathways both singly and interactively.[43]

Redefining Disease

A fourth sign of change is the expanding definition of disease. Interestingly, this change can be seen both as a reinforcement of reductionist thinking and as a step forward for environmentalism. Environmental disease is usually construed (as is all disease) as clinical illness. In recent years, however, certain investigators, some of them associated with mainstream environmental groups, have defined environmental disease as the minute physiological abnormalities that are sometimes discovered in people who live with pollution. These abnormalities are called biomarkers. They are found in samples of blood or adipose tissue or breast milk or other media.[44] Classically, investigators divide biomarkers into three types: those that indicate exposure, those that indicate susceptibility, and those that indicate disease. But as the National Research Council points out, "there is a continuum between markers of exposure and markers of health status."[45] The abnormalities caused by exposure to hazardous substances—the biomarkers for exposure—can also be understood as the first symptoms of disease. In this case, disease becomes a sequence of indicators over time instead of a fixed clinical illness, so it is possible to identify environmental illness early. In the words of the National Research Council, biomarker research is a "fuller method," compared with the "current method of estimating risks by relating exposure to clinical disease (morbidity and mortality).... As a result, health events are less likely to be viewed as binary phenomena (presence or absence of disease) than they are to be seen as a series of changes on a continuum—through homeostatic adaptation, dysfunction, to disease and death."[46]

Biomarker research offers great advantages to investigators making health assessments at hazardous waste sites. First, they do not have to wait until residents get sick. With sophisticated biomarker research methods, they can identify cardiopulmonary disorders or tumors or reproductive problems at their very beginning. Second, when investigators compare health problems in exposed and unexposed groups of people, they do not have to rely on guesses based on mathematical modeling or on extrapolations from soil or water or air samples or on questionnaires to know who goes in which group. They are therefore less likely to weaken the power of their studies by mistakenly including large numbers of unexposed people in a group of presumedly exposed people. Thus, where pollution has had a health effect, investigators are more likely to be able to show it.[47] As a result, environmental and health agencies are more likely to take action.

Research on the health effects of exposure to lead provides a good example. Until the 1950s, scientists had no convincing way to reject the lead industry's claims that lead in the environment occurred naturally, that the average levels in blood were safe, and that the only serious problems were rare, accidental, acute poisonings. But as biomarker technology was developed, a group of politically progressive clinicians and epidemiologists began examining blood samples from children in urban neighborhoods in Boston and New York. They were eventually able to correlate high blood-lead levels with learning disabilities, hyperactivity, school failure, and mental retardation. They were also able to correlate high blood-lead levels with exposures to automobile exhausts and paint.[48] So clear is this correlation that today when researchers do health studies where children are exposed to lead they do not have to show that the children have any clinical illness or observable learning problems, only that they have high levels of lead in their blood. This condition itself is a disease. It is called lead poisoning. And because it is relatively easy to link environmental lead with blood abnormalities, and the blood abnormalities with mental and physical illnesses, the EPA's usual critics (with the exception of the lead industry) rarely include lead in their lists of unnecessary regulations.

Biomarker research can also work for certain synthetic chemicals. As I note in Chapter One, when the EPA needed more convincing evidence at Love Canal that exposure to the leaking landfill was a health hazard, it commissioned a chromosome study. The scientist doing the study examined blood samples from thirty-six residents for breaks in the normal chromosome structure. As it turned out, the study had technical flaws that rendered it useless to the EPA[49] and a later, differently designed study by the Centers for Disease Control found no relationship between chromosomal damage and exposure to Love Canal.[50] Biomarker investigations at other sites, however, have been more useful to environmentalists, notably studies of Woburn, Massachusetts, residents exposed to drinking water contaminated with trichloroethylene (TCE).[51]

Biomarker research does have important drawbacks. From a pragmatic perspective, biomarkers are limited sources of information. They do not occur in all diseases or in all persons, and they can be caused by other things besides chemicals. From an ethical perspective, biomarkers raise serious questions. For example: Should people with abnormal markers be told? Should they be barred from certain jobs, refused health insurance, counseled not to have children? From an environmentalist perspective, biomarker research is excessively reductionistic. It easily leads to a focus on high-risk individuals instead of on high-risk environments.[52]

These are all important criticisms. Nevertheless a focus on minute bodily reactions to environmental toxins can expand the definition of disease beyond clinical illness. And it can thereby rescue environmental epidemiologists from having to show that the people they study have health problems in the traditional meaning of the term. Epidemiologists have to show only that people's bodies have started reacting to exposure—that the long disease process has begun.

Standard of Proof

A fifth sign of change toward a more environmentalist science is the disquiet some scientists express about epidemiology's validity rules. Despite what most laypeople might imagine, environmental epidemiologists do not directly ask whether exposure to pollution has caused disease. Instead, they go about it backwards, always starting with a negative hypothesis: that there is *no* correlation between exposure and disease. Every study's aim is to disprove that hypothesis. The disproof demands a high level of certainty. Investigators must show, using a standard mathematical formula, that no more than a 5 percent probability exists that their findings could be the result of chance. In other words, epidemiologists must be 95 percent sure before they will conclude that a correlation exists between exposure and disease.

Obviously, the high standard biases epidemiology toward the status quo. It is change that must be justified, not a continuation of current exposures. And the justification is not easy to come by. The inherent weaknesses in environmental epidemiology that I describe in Chapter Two make it hard for studies of small populations to find much environmentally related disease. Even when studies detect a big increase in disease rates, there is seldom a scientific rationale for reducing pollution levels because the studies discovering the problem are not 95 percent certain.

Faced with this situation, some scientists and philosophers of science argue that statistical significance should not be confused with public health significance: that what is good for science is not necessarily good for regulation.[53] It is important to be 95 percent certain of your results if your aim is to add to scientific knowledge about the link between a suspect substance and disease—research that Carl Cranor calls "science for its own sake."[54] But if your aim is to protect public health, and a high standard of mathematical certainty both robs you of a scientific rationale for doing so and justifies those who would expose the public to potentially harmful substances, the standard is unethical. In the words of biologist Beverly Paigen:

> Before Love Canal I also needed to have 95 percent certainty before I was convinced of a result. But seeing this rigorously applied in a situation where the consequences of an error meant that pregnancies were resulting in miscarriages, stillbirths, and children with medical problems, I realized I was making a value judgement. In other issues of public health and safety—bomb threats, possible epidemics, etc.—we do not insist on 95 percent probability of harmful consequences before action is taken. Why is that the criterion in environmental health?[55]

The adoption of a lower criterion—say 75 percent or even 51 percent—in studies with public health import would, obviously, increase the number of studies that could be deemed statistically significant. The increase would reinforce environmentalist principles by providing more scientific proof that interference in nature is harmful. At the same time, it would subvert the position of anti-environmentalists who use the lack of positive health studies to argue that current levels of pollution are safe.

A lower criterion would also switch the burden of risk from the general public to industry. A high standard of statistical significance creates a relatively large number of false negatives—studies erroneously concluding that a suspect substance is safe. False negatives provide no scientific justification for protecting the public's health even though the public faces risks. In contrast, a low standard of significance creates a relatively large number of false positives—studies erroneously concluding that a suspect substance is dangerous. False positives provide a scientific rationale for requiring industries to change their waste disposal methods even though the change is not necessary.[56] In other words, there is no way to be neutral about mathematical criteria when they are used to evaluate studies of the health effects of environmental pollution. If you demand a high standard of proof before calling a study valid, you automatically side with the industry that produces the substance. If you accept a lower standard of proof, you side with the community exposed to it. The new attention to this reality has not brought a clamor for change in the validity rules. The attention does, however, provide environmentalists with a rationale for embracing statistically weak studies.

If science reflects the culture in which scientists live, then as cultures change so should science. We have seen indications of an important cultural change as increasing numbers of people agree with environmentalists that nature is a fragile, interconnected, organic whole, vulnerable to harm from nonnatural things. It is still too early to know for sure that this cultural change will fundamentally affect the environmental health sciences. But some environmental epidemiologists are designing innovative ways to study the effects of industrial toxins on public health, ways that are less reductionist than traditional epidemiology and less reflective of the old assumption that nature is basically strong and sturdy. In consequence, increasing numbers of studies are showing a positive correlation between a community's diseases and its exposure to environmental pollution.

It is important to point out that the authors of these new studies are not necessarily passive receivers of environmentalist ideas. Many of the scientists identified in this chapter are active participants in the environmental movement. (They work for environmental organizations; they write articles for publications that explicitly identify with the movement's goals; they speak at movement events.) This state of affairs seldom gets attention from scholars examining the effect of culture on science. Social constructivists tend to portray scientists as living in a sea of unexamined cultural assumptions that they involuntarily replicate in their research. But in periods of social change, when the old assumptions are contested, scientists are more likely to pay attention to the ideas guiding their work. If they find incongruities between what they hold true about the world and the regular practices in their field, they are apt to search for new ways to do their investigations. In the case of environmental epidemiology, we have seen scientists, many of whom publically identify with the environmental movement, consciously trying to do studies that will show the great harm that is likely to occur when people treat nature as a mere means to an end. That is, like all scientists, they assume that their job is to describe reality to the best of their ability.

Recognizing the work that some epidemiologists are doing to develop a science more in keeping with environmentalist principles suggests two kinds of relations between culture and science. In one, described by scholars such as Keller, Haraway, Martin, and Krieger and Fee, scientists unconsciously design studies that reproduce undemocratic and inegalitarian values. The bias in their research goes largely unnoticed as long as the values are uncontested. In another, the kind I describe in this chapter, scientists struggle to invent ways to investigate the world that will be consistent with new democratic, egalitarian (or in this case, environmentalist) values. The bias in these investigations is more likely to be noticed both because the underlying values are new and because the results often imply the need for new public policies.[57]

Of course the results do not always do so. In the case of environmental epidemiology, if a suspect pollutant or group of pollutants is not actually harmful to health, even environmentalist investigators will eventually discover that it is safe, as long as their research projects are careful and honest. By the same token, careful studies on environmental pollutants by industry scientists sometimes show those pollutants to be hazardous. In other words, the actual properties of chemicals are not infinitely malleable by values. My point in this chapter has been that values influence scientists, not that values predetermine the outcome of research.

The next chapter concentrates on the people who have the most to gain from studies showing that environmental pollution endangers health. I look again at the citizens' groups that protest exposure to pollution, and this time I consider their relations with the government agencies that are responsible for protecting citizens from environmental toxins.

5 Understanding Risk

The new developments in environmental health science have not, so far, had enough bearing on environmental policy to lessen citizen protest. If anything, the number of groups fighting exposure to environmental toxins has probably grown substantially in the last decade. It is impossible to make any kind of accurate count of grassroots environmental groups,[1] but clearly they have become a force to contend with, especially for state and local government agencies responsible for health and the environment. In a talk I once gave to the Southeast Michigan Health Association—whose members are county health department officials—I repeated one published estimate of eight thousand grassroots environmental groups in the United States. The estimate met with skepticism. "There're a lot more than that," joked one man in the back. "I have eight thousand in my county alone." People looked at him and chuckled appreciatively. He had reminded everybody of the pressure they faced on the job. The men and women in the audience were the people community groups argue with at public hearings, deluge with demands, picket, and threaten to sue.[2]

Among the results of this pressure on government has been the publication of guidelines for dealing with community activists. The guidelines all address a single question: What should agency personnel do when one group of people insists that an abandoned dump or a waste incinerator in their community poses a serious public health hazard, while another group contends that these things are safe? The question is similar to the one I submit at the end of Chapter One. But there I was vaguer about the owner of the problem. After describing struggles in Connecticut, Oregon, and New York to prevent exposure to environmental pollution, and after showing that in each case scientific evidence showed that the exposure was safe, I ask "How should we respond to these three stories?" In the next three chapters I state that "we" should realize that the research subverting grassroots groups' claims is at least partly a consequence of the pre-environmentalist assumptions that infuse scientific investigations. Implicit in my assertion is that one way people can respond to grassroots groups' protests is to foster environmentalist principles (if they want to support environmental activism) or to denigrate the principles (if they want to thwart this kind of activism).

In this chapter I focus on government agencies' response to competing claims about environmental pollution and what citizens do and can do about that response. I argue that the scholars who study debates over the toxicity of environmental pollution and the administrators who deal with the parties to these debates misunderstand the central problem. They see the debates as conflicts between experts and laypeople—experts taking the position that exposures to environmental pollutants are safe, laypeople saying the exposures are dangerous.[3] But the expert-lay dichotomy is false. Citizens who resist exposure to pollution are not isolated from expert opinion. They draw heavily on the expertise of environmentalist scientists like those I cite in Chapter Four. These scientists teach them about the health effects of pollution and help them collect new data.

Risk Perception

The idea that debates over the hazardousness of environmental pollution are controversies between experts and laypeople has its firmest empirical foundation in the work of Paul Slovic and his colleagues and followers. Since the late 1970s, these researchers, most of them cognitive psychologists, have been studying what they call risk perception. In dozens of published papers they have shown that experts and laypeople estimate the risks of dying from environmental hazards very differently and use different kinds of rationality in making those estimates.[4]

In the initial demonstration that experts and laypeople construe risk differently, Slovic, Baruch Fischhoff, and Sarah Lichtenstein asked three groups of ordinary people to estimate death rates from various modern technologies. The researchers then compared these estimates with the estimates by a group of "experts"—people with "professional involvement in risk assessment." They found that for nuclear power, pesticides, and some other technologies, laypeople estimated death rates as far higher than they actually are, while experts made more-accurate estimates. But instead of simply maligning laypeople for being irrational, Slovic and his colleagues set out to understand laypeople's thinking. They hypothesized that laypeople think of hazards not according to expected fatalities but according to the attributes of the hazards. So they administered a new questionnaire that listed attributes. They found that the hazards ordinary folk find very risky have two characteristics. They are "unknown"; that is, they are unobservable, are unfamiliar, have delayed effects, and so on. And they are "dread"; that is, they are uncontrollable, involuntary, inequitably distributed, and so on. Among the hazards in this latter category are radioactive waste, dioxin, and DNA technology. In contrast, the hazards people find not very risky are just the opposite: observable and familiar, controllable and voluntary. Among these hazards are bicycles, chainsaws, and elevators.[5]

The researchers concluded that laypeople are not ignorant of what is "really" risky. Rather, compared with experts, they employ a broader and richer kind of rationality. Instead of viewing hazards from a reductionist, technical perspective, they take into consideration qualitative issues such as fairness and equity. (Is everyone at equal risk from the hazard?) They are concerned with costs and benefits. (Does the hazard help ordinary people in some way?) They think about social cohesion. (Would an accident destroy my community?) They consider future generations. (Could unborn children be affected?) In sum, they bring their values into play.[6]

This research has been enormously helpful to scholars sympathetic to grassroots organizing as well as to grassroots activists themselves. It provides an answer to the charge that ordinary citizens are witless, hysterical, or uneducated when it comes to environmental pollution, and it bestows a new dignity on their mobilization. In so doing, it gives government agency personnel a reason besides the simple imperative of democracy to listen to the citizenry. But if experts, to whom governments also listen, disagree with citizens about what is harmful, how much and in what ways should citizens' perceptions of danger influence policy decisions?

Risk Communication

The risk literature offers two kinds of answers. Both are under the rubric of "risk communication," and both appear in the guidelines offered to

agency personnel.[7] Some scholars think that, although citizens' efforts
to affect government should be respected, the goal of risk communication is to bring the citizens' ideas about risk closer to the experts'. A
major theme in these risk communication guidelines is that agencies
need to gain proficiency in education techniques.[8]

As James Flynn, Paul Slovic, and C.K. Mertz put it after describing
the public's profound skepticism about the safety of burying high-level
nuclear waste at Yucca Mountain, "Countering such attitudes and opinions will require extraordinary honesty, patience, and skill in communicating the appropriate information to the public."[9] This way of construing risk communication reflects the prudent notion that
environmental policies should be based on sound science. It assumes,
however, that the agency's task is to reduce citizen protest, not to reduce
environmental pollutants. In K. S. Shrader-Frechette's words, risk communication practioners "ask how to mitigate the impact of risk *perceptions* (which they assume to be erroneous), rather than how to mitigate
the impact of *risk* itself."[10]

A second answer says that citizens have something to add to administrative decision making. In this view, citizens' perceptions of risk, although stemming from a kind of rationality distinct from the experts',
are equally as legitimate. In Peter Sandman's words, "[T]echnical professionals are the experts on what's hazardous and what isn't... citizens
are the experts on what's outrageous and what isn't."[11] Risk communication, then, should be a two-way process in which agency personnel bring
in technical data and citizens bring in social values.[12] Certainly this
sounds like good advice. Two-way risk communication, in which citizens
have a genuine role, is more democratic than one-way communication
in which agency people lecture citizens. But none of these guidelines
makes clear what agency personnel are supposed to do once they have
listened to citizens. Agencies would appear to have three unsatisfactory
choices. (1) They can hear citizens explain why they think the exposure
in question is dangerous but support environmental policies consistent
with the experts' view that it is not a choice that replicates one-way communication and abrogates the claim that citizens' risk perceptions are legitimate and valuable. (2) They can accept citizens' reasoning about
what is dangerous and protect them from environmental exposures
even when the experts say that the exposures are harmless, a choice implying that environmental decisions should be based on what people be-

lieve instead of on what scientists know. (3) Or they can work out some compromise policy that does not protect people as much as people want to be protected but does not entirely negate scientific research either, a choice likely to satisfy no one.

Facing these dismal alternatives, however, may be less an inevitable dilemma than an artifact of the small stage on which the risk communication literature presents the situation. Most of it depicts a highly circumscribed event: alarmed citizens fighting against the siting of a waste treatment facility or the practices of a polluting industry. But people's attempts to influence environmental policies occur in many more arenas. To find out what they are, one need only look at the scholarly writings on citizen participation. An inquiry based on this literature suggests different understandings of risk perception and questions the validity of the central concept in risk communication guidelines: the citizen-expert dichotomy.

As the previous chapter shows, the logic of the citizen-expert dichotomy has already been weakened by scholars who take the constructionist view that scientific research inevitably reflects the society in which scientists work. These scholars argue that facts and values are inevitably linked; scientists can neither form nor test theories without appealing to extrascientific assumptions. Some scholars have applied constructionism to risk perception. They say it is naive to assume that experts *know* what is a hazard while citizens only *perceive* hazards, for experts have no choice but to combine empirical observations and value judgments.[13] Paul Slovic himself has joined the constructionist scholars. In a recent essay, he wrote that experts' assessment of risk "is inherently subjective and represents a blending of science and judgment with important psychological, social, cultural, and political factors."[14]

But I criticize the dualism in the risk perception literature from the other side, too. Just as most of the literature oversimplifies the concept of expert by assuming that experts deal only in facts, so it oversimplifies the concept of citizen by assuming that citizens deal only in values. Researchers make this mistake about citizens, I contend, by ignoring the organized groups through which citizens influence environmental decisions and from which citizens get many of their ideas about what is dangerous. They thus confuse "citizen" with "individual" and fail to ask about the expertise used by the organizations that actually represent citizens to policy makers.

Citizen Participation

The literature on citizen participation identifies three avenues available to people who hope to influence the government: the electoral process, the policy-making process, and the agenda-setting process. In the electoral process, citizens participate by voting and its attendant activities, such as working for candidates or sending them money.[15] In the policy-making process citizens participate in more varied ways. One is to lobby elected officials or executive agency personnel by writing letters, talking with politicians and their staff, providing technical information, testifying at hearings, signing petitions, and taking part in rallies or demonstrations.[16] Another is to file lawsuits.[17] A third is to serve on administrative agency-initiated advisory panels, commissions, and boards, and a fourth is to testify at agency-sponsored public hearings and meetings.[18] In the agenda-setting process, citizens participate in more subtle ways. They try to affect what the public construes as a political problem and thus what the government is called upon to address. This sort of citizen participation employs a wide variety of means, including skillful use of the media, to reframe and thus draw new attention to old issues or to transform accepted conditions into contested ones.[19]

The most important point, in the context of the risk literature, about these three ways to affect government is that citizens can participate effectively as individuals only when they vote or send money to candidates. In other aspects of the electoral process, and in the policy-making and agenda-setting processes, citizens usually have to organize into groups to have much influence. The strange thing about the risk literature is that it misses this point. Despite its recognition that people are socially embedded perceivers of risk, and despite its concern with the best way administrators can respond to organized citizens, the literature takes the individual citizen, not the groups that citizens belong to, as the unit of analysis. This formulation causes risk scholars to ignore the activities and the composition of the organizations through which most activist citizens acquire information about environmental hazards. They thus misconstrue the actual relation between citizens and experts.

I am not suggesting that risk perception research has completely neglected organized groups. The initial studies in the field surveyed members of the League of Women Voters and members of a business and professional organization.[20] But in the many publications that risk perception researchers have generated from those studies there is no indication that the researchers see the "members" as anything but proxies for the public at large. In fact, some scholars criticize them for not representing the general public well enough. Some critics have done new studies in order to form a more accurate picture of the average person's beliefs.[21] Certainly it is interesting to know how the typical American perceives risk. But we care what people think about risk mainly because they try to influence government decisions. Thus, studies of individuals are not enough. We also need inquiries in which the unit of analysis is the organizations through which citizens participate.

To check my statement that most citizens participate in government via groups, consider first the policy-making process. Although many individuals do become angry or worried (or heartened) by political events and, all on their own, write letters or make phone calls encouraging government officials to act, most constituent messages received in government offices are stimulated by organized groups.[22] Moreover, especially on the federal level, it is seldom individual, unaffiliated citizens who testify at hearings or public meetings, talk with elected representatives and their aides or with agency personnel, and provide technical information to legislators or to bureaucrats. More often it is the paid staff, the consultants, or high-visibility volunteers (movie stars, for example) representing the organized groups who actually do the work. In these cases, not only do citizens participate as members of groups instead of as individuals, but other people carry out the participation for them.[23] The group nature of citizen participation is also illustrated when citizens sign petitions and attend rallies, demonstrations, and other crowd events—all activities requiring organized groups. And, although lawsuits with policy implications sometimes carry the name of a single individual, participation by litigation is usually done through formally organized groups.[24]

The group nature of citizenship is less clearly illustrated in the case of advisory boards and public meetings. Sometimes, citizen members of advisory boards specifically represent existing grassroots groups; sometimes they represent community-based organizations; and sometimes they represent the public at large.[25] There are apparently no data showing which kinds of representation are most common. Similarly, it is hard to know what percent of public meetings and hearings are attended mainly by unaffiliated members of the general public and what percent are attended primarily by people specifically supporting an organized group. Without more data, we can only conclude that on boards and at public meetings, citizens are sometimes formally unaffiliated and sometimes formally representative of organized groups.

The concept of unaffiliated citizen, however, fails to recognize that organized groups affect citizens' ideas. In other words, it ignores another critical way that people can influence government: the process of agenda setting. Although occasionally individual citizens can change what the public, and the government, construes as a political problem— consider the attention Michael Harrington brought to poverty in *The Other America*, the effect of Ralph Nader's *Unsafe at Any Speed*, and of course, the power of *Silent Spring*—for the most part, if you want to change the public agenda you have to join a group.

Work by members of feminist organizations has been a major factor in the transformation in public opinion about women's role in society.[26] The activities of civil rights groups fostered new cultural ideals about racial equality.[27] A crusade by environmental organizations got Americans to think that destruction of the Amazon rain forest constitutes a public problem.[28] In these and other campaigns, members of organized groups redefined an accepted condition or situation as a political problem and worked to get the public to embrace the new definition. Once the groups were successful, the newly defined problem became a legitimate arena for government policy making.

It is important to observe that organized groups cannot take all the credit for setting new political agendas. I suggest in Chapter Three and argue more explicitly in Chapter Seven, that the "forces" affecting change are far greater than formal associations of activist citizens. In this chapter I focus on group activities, however, because my question is how ordinary citizens can most effectively influence government.

It is no mystery why people participate in policy making and agenda setting primarily through organized groups. For policy making, the unaffiliated average citizen has a hard time learning what is going on, whom to contact, and where to get useful information because modern government is so complex.[29] Few individuals have the scientific and technical training necessary to study the immense amount of data accompanying important issues.[30] For agenda setting, most lone amateurs simply lack the resources to construct new social issues.[31] Perhaps most important, citizens seldom enter politics on an empty stage. Businesses are already there. Although their main energies go into the production of goods or services, large successful businesses also employ lobbyists and run information campaigns in the expectation of getting some control over the policies that affect them. To have comparable influence, citizens must also organize sizable and powerful groups.[32]

If, then, we care what citizens think about risk because their opinions influence government decisions, and if citizens influence those decisions primarily through organized groups, the interesting question in risk perception is not about individuals. Instead of asking what reasoning individual people use to decide that a technology or a situation or a substance is hazardous, we need to ask what reasoning organized groups use. To answer the question, I turn first to the Natural Resources Defense Council and its conclusion that Alar is dangerous. I use the Alar story because it is so frequently cited to illustrate laypeople's unscientific rationality.[33]

Influencing the Federal Government

As I noted in the introductory chapter to this book, the Natural Resources Defense Council (NRDC) is one of the dozen or so "mainstream" environmental organizations that citizens can join if they want to influence national environmental policy. Through NRDC, as through any citizens' group, citizens can lobby members of Congress, pressure bureaucrats at the EPA, testify at congressional hearings, sue violators of environmental laws and regulations, and spread information to the general public about environmental hazards.[34] NRDC specifically solicits members on the basis that they cannot do those things alone. In the words of one recruiting letter, "You have heard a lot of talk these days about the powerlessness of citizens. The 'experts' say people can't be heard.... [But our record is] a compelling story of how concerned and organized citizens made a world of difference." Another letter, sent over the signature of a prominent member, says, "Citizens like us cannot change government policies and defend our natural heritage unless we have clout. That's where NRDC comes in."[35]

In early 1989 NRDC caused a whirlwind of media stories, consumer fear, and industry fury by announcing that preschool children are at high risk for cancers and neurological disorders because they ingest high levels of pesticides along with their fruits and vegetables. The announcement came initially in an emotional story on CBS's *60 Minutes* that focused on a single registered pesticide, a growth hormone called Alar.[36] Alar was licensed for use on apples, so residues showed up in apple juice, apple sauce, and on the raw fruit itself—all common foods in American children's diets. The public responded to the *60 Minutes* segment and to the print media coverage of the NRDC report by refusing to buy apples and apple products. Public pressure was so great that several cities (including Los Angles and New York) took apples out of school cafeterias; supermarkets put up "No Alar" signs; and Congress considered legislation that would ban Alar. After three months, the EPA issued a preliminary determination to cancel the use of Alar on all foods. Six months after that, the company producing Alar voluntarily withdrew its registration.[37]

The whole affair generated an intense attack on NRDC by a number of scientists. Joseph Rosen at Rutgers University accused NRDC of using dubious toxicological data, misrepresenting Alar's breakdown product as a genotoxin, incorrectly estimating apple consumption, and relying only on worst-case scenarios.[38] In congressional testimony, Frank Young from the FDA insisted that "there is not a significant risk at this time facing the American people in the consumption of apples."[39] John Moore from the EPA said, "The public is being led [by the NRDC report] to believe that...their children are at very high cancer risk due to Alar residues in apples and apple products. This is simply not true."[40] Scientists at the National Food Processors Association faulted the NRDC report for every one of its claims. Their spokesperson charged, "The basic conclusions of the NRDC report rest on stringing together a series of improbable 'worst case' assumptions and/or speculations. In all of these areas, NRDC has either gotten its facts wrong or has made methodological errors."[41] And a less economically interested body of scientists, a committee made up of representatives from the World Health Organization and the Food and Agriculture Organization, reviewed the scientific data and announced that Alar is not a carcinogen even at fairly high levels of exposure.[42]

As these excerpts from the controversy show, it is possible to make the Alar case look like one in which citizens, acting through or inspired by an interest group, press Congress and the bureaucracy to make new policies, while experts criticize the logic underlying the citizens' position. But the controversy cannot accurately be characterized as a split between experts and citizens. In the first place, the NRDC study used only data from U.S. government scientists. In the second place, it was done by just the sort of people Slovic and his colleagues designated as experts. In the third place, people outside of the NRDC who were also "experts" publicly endorsed the NRDC position. Let me elaborate.

NRDC's announcement about the danger of pesticide exposure to children followed the completion of a two-year study reported in the

1989 publication *Intolerable Risk: Pesticides in Our Children's Food.*[43] The report was a fairly dense technical treatise, 136 pages long, with twenty-two tables, ten figures, three appendixes, and 220 endnotes. It started by describing two sets of data, both acquired from the EPA. One listed the consumption rates for the twenty-seven food items most frequently eaten by preschoolers. These data showed that children, compared with adults, eat more food relative to body weight and that their consumption patterns had changed significantly in recent years. The other data set listed the residue levels of twenty-three pesticides known to have health effects and commonly detected in the twenty-seven food items. Combining these two data sets, *Intolerable Risk* calculated the amount of hazardous pesticides to which preschoolers were exposed in their food. The next step was to assess the health outcome from this exposure. The report used the results of animal bioassays, considered in its calculation the long latency period between exposure and cancer, and concluded that between 5,500 and 6,200 "of the current population of American preschoolers may eventually get cancer solely as a result of their exposure before six years of age to eight pesticides or metabolites commonly found in fruits and vegetables."[44]

As for the people who did the study, they were (as were the "experts" Slovic and his colleagues interviewed) people with "professional involvement in risk assessment." In Slovic's risk perception studies, these included a geographer, an economist, a lawyer, a biologist, a biochemist, a government regulator, and an environmental policy analyst.[45] In the NRDC study, they included a public health professional, a computer programmer, a physicist, an economist, a general scientist, and four lawyers.

The principal authors listed in *Intolerable Risk* are Bradford Sewell and Robin Whyatt, both then NRDC staff members. At the time of the report, Whyatt had a master's degree in public health and fifteen years of experience with toxic substances, first as executive director of Scenic Hudson and then at NRDC. Sewell had an undergraduate degree in human biology, two years of experience working on an earlier NRDC toxics project, and skill in computer programming.[46] Whyatt and Sewell were aided by Glen Gilchrist, a consultant to the project, who developed the basic computer modeling system for exposure assessment.

The person responsible for performing the crucial carcinogenic risk assessments was another consultant, William Nicholson from the Department of Environmental Medicine at Mount Sinai School of Medicine. Nicholson, whose doctorate is in physics, began developing assessment models in 1980. Before the pesticide project at NRDC he had written criteria documents on asbestos for the EPA and for the Swedish government. He had developed a risk assessment model for asbestos for the U.S. Occupational Safety and Health Administration that the agency continues to use, and he had done extensive reviews of PCB cancer risk for a government agency in Ontario.

The overall editor of the report was Lawrie Mott, who holds a master's degree in general science from Yale and had had nine years of experience in pesticides at NRDC. She had also served as a member of the EPA Administrator's Pesticide Advisory Committee and had sat on the California Department of Health's Cancer Policy Review Committee. Four NRDC lawyers worked on the report: Janet Hathaway, Jane Bloom, Jacqueline Warren, and Albert Meyerhoff. They have all served as official members of various EPA advisory committees on the regulation of toxic substances.[47]

During the time they were working on the report, the authors consulted with other "professionals in risk assessment." Some, like John Wargo at Yale and Richard Wiles at the Center for Resource Economics, were "shadow advisors" unacknowledged in the final report. The most visible outside specialists were the nine official peer reviewers: four M.D.s, four Ph.D.s, and one Ed.D.[48]

There are several indications that the final product also met the approval of "experts" unconnected to NRDC. In Congressional hearing, both Deborah Prothrow-Stith, commissioner of the Massachusetts Department of Health, and Richard Jackson, chairman of the Committee on Environmental Hazards of the American Academy of Pediatrics, supported NRDC's conclusion that children's health was endangered from pesticide residues in food and urged the EPA to adopt stronger regulations.[49] Later, a team of researchers from the California Department of Health Services argued that NRDC could have made an even stronger case that exposure to Alar puts children at risk for cancer.[50] And four years after *Intolerable Risk,* the National Research Council published a study corroborating NRDC's major conclusions. The National Research Council's study shows that age-related differences in susceptibility to pesticides exist, that children's diets differ significantly from adults' thereby exposing them to greater amounts of pesticides, and that these early exposures are potentially harmful.[51]

One might respond to all of this—the statement that *Intolerable Risk* used only data provided by federal agencies, the assertion that those responsible for the report fit the category of experts, the citing of corroborating experts—by asking whether the NRDC report was reliable. Did NRDC do "good science"? But that would be the wrong question here, for excellence is not the point of this story. The point is rather that NRDC, one of the citizens' organizations through which ordinary people work to influence environmental policy, did not perceive the risks of pesticides by using a special form of reasoning. NRDC did not conclude that Alar is hazardous because Alar is "unknown" and "dread." It did not publish an ethical treatise calling Alar dangerous because exposure is involuntary, hidden, and uncontrollable. It did not bring up values such as fairness and equity. Instead, NRDC used the same kind of reductionist, scientific rationality that Slovic and his colleagues labeled "expert," and finding that between 5,500 and 6,200 preschoolers at the time might eventually get cancer from dietary exposure to pesticides, deduced that exposure was hazardous. It then pressed for government action.

This story suggests that, in the experience of federal policy makers, citizens are indistinguishable from experts. Private citizens rarely express their opinions on the hazards of environmental toxins directly to the federal government. Instead, they combine with like-minded folk and hire experts to do it for them. And as the NRDC case illustrates, they sometimes also hire experts to develop the knowledge on which those opinions are based. Even when citizens' groups like the NRDC do not actually do research—that is, even when they take positions based on literature reviews (which is more frequently the case)—they depend on experts. Thus, most of the time when policy makers hear from "citizens"—via lobbies, lawsuits, or advisory panels and public hearings—the citizens are representing experts. This is not to deny that the average person evaluates risk differently from a professional in risk assessment. It is to call attention to the difference between the average person, the one reflected in risk perception questionnaires, and the citizen, the one trying to influence government through the mediation of a group. And it is to suggest that the risk communication scholars have it wrong: when governments hear opposing judgments about the dangers of a technology, the two sides represent not laypeople and experts but two groups of experts.

Influencing State and Local Government

But one might claim that the Natural Resources Defense Council is not the kind of citizens' group that counts in a discussion of risk perception and risk communication. While conceding that some citizens join mainstream groups in order to influence national environmental policy, one might point out that risk communicators usually meet with quite different citizens, that is, those organized into neighborhood environmental groups such as the Love Canal Homeowners Association and CATS (Citizens Against Toxic Sprays). Neighborhood groups are concerned with local and state policies and rarely have scientists on staff. Indeed, by definition, they seldom have staffs at all. It is the people in these groups, one might argue, whose reasoning about hazards differs from experts' and who depend on subjective values more than on objective science.

This objection to the focus on NRDC, however, ignores the agenda-setting aspects of citizen participation. It assumes that participation by mainstream groups has no effect on grassroots groups or on members of the general public not (yet) formed into any such group. The assumption is erroneous. From a policy-making perspective, what the NRDC did in the Alar case was to get one registered pesticide off the market. From an agenda-setting perspective, it underscored and rebroadcast a message that environmentalists had been promoting since *Silent Spring:* synthetic chemicals can be harmful to the environment and to public health. One reason the NRDC study on pesticides is important is that it is partly responsible for people's beliefs about environmental risk. It added new particulars to general information that was already available but that the risk perception researchers had failed to notice. Instead of starting from the assumption that people think a technology is risky because they have heard experts say so, the researchers started from the assumption that people think a technology is risky because it has certain characteristics. The researchers never asked their respondents about the source of their views about risk, and they never asked themselves who or what assigns characteristics to a technology. In short, the risk perception research ignores the existence of the environmental movement.

Importantly, the movement's message is not simply that synthetic chemicals are dangerous. It is also that *scientists* think they are. The movement thus locates environmental protest in the realm of provable hypotheses, of cause-and-effect research, of objective knowledge. It didn't have to. As the risk perception studies suggest, environmental activism can avoid emphasizing science. Opposition to pollution can be situated in a moral realm, justified on the basis that exposure violates social values such as personal control, fairness, and community cohesion. However, environmentalists have emphasized science since the beginning of the movement. So when grassroots groups began forming in the 1970s to protest pollution, there was an already-existing, widely used framework within which they could position their complaints.

At least five pieces of evidence indicate that grassroots groups have used that framework. The first piece of evidence comes from the organizing manuals directed at community-level environmental organizations. Most of these manuals are produced by the grassroots support groups I describe in the Overview. The manuals share a basic premise: scientists know what is hazardous and citizens need that knowledge too. The manuals list the government agencies from which citizens can get toxicological, epidemiological, and regulatory information. They direct readers to peer-reviewed scientific journals, suggest they attend professional meetings, and in some cases advise them to contact scientists directly. They explain how to use the Freedom of Information Act and the Community Right to Know provisions of the Superfund law in order to get data from polluting industries. They show how to find and use computer databases. They tell about private organizations that publish information on toxics.[52]

A second piece of evidence that grassroots groups locate their protests in a scientific framework is the existence of two movement publications that pass scientific findings on to environmental activists. The better-known in grassroots circles is *RACHEL's Environment and Health Weekly*, an independent publication put out by Peter Montague and available both electronically and by mail. Started in 1983, *RACHEL's* now consists of a five- or six-page essay on a current issue in environmental science, heavily referencing the academic literature. The other is the *Environmental Health Monthly*, a newsletter put out by the Center for Health, Environment and Justice, currently the major grassroots support group. Begun in 1988, the newsletter reprints in each issue one or more articles in their entirety from the peer-reviewed scientific literature, along with a page or so of commentary. Both publications concentrate on new research indicating that environmental pollution endangers human health.

A third piece of evidence is Nicholas Freudenberg's survey of 242 grassroots environmental groups. "More than half the respondents," he writes, "reported that they attended conferences or meetings with scientific experts, read government reports, met with activists from other local or national environmental groups, read newspaper articles in order to educate themselves." Notably, the respondents held the information from scientists in higher esteem than that from their fellow environmental activists: "Contact with scientific experts was rated to be the most valuable source of information (41 percent of the groups), followed by reviews of government records or reports (33 percent) and conversations with other environmental activists (29 percent)."[53]

My own interviews corroborate Freudenberg's survey. For example, Lynne Ide at the Connecticut Citizens Action Group told me, "Our members get a lot of scientific information. They are just... rabid about all this stuff.... If you talk to any of them at the meetings, if you go to their houses, they have journals, and they are reading everything they can get through the mail. There is this whole underground network of people... and they send each other all this stuff."[54] Stephen Lester, the science director at the Center of Health, Environment and Justice said, "One of the biggest mistakes the professionals make is to underestimate the science that these community groups can learn. They are voracious learners. They really want to know the science.... There is a steep learning curve. They move quickly up the curve. They know a lot more every week from what they knew the week before. Not everyone, of course, but the core members."[55] And, when I talked with Jerry Poje at the World Wildlife Fund, he said,

> As a university professor I had a damn lot of trouble trying to explain to upper-middle-class kids about environmental biology, environmental fate, environmental chemistry. But when it came to talking to housewives at the Superfund site, it was very easy to explain what environmental fate was, about the mobilities of the various chemicals in the environment. People were very able to understand. It's the threat posed to people that gets them to think further from their own information base.[56]

A fourth piece of evidence comes from case studies of local struggles like the ones I recount in Chapter One. At Love Canal, when the New York Department of Health maintained that only a few people were at risk the leaking landfill, the citizens' group turned to a cancer researcher at Rosewell Park Memorial Institute who helped them gather the health data that eventually justified their relocation.[57] At Alsea, when the Forest Service denied that pesticide spray endangered human health, the local residents got help and advice "from scientists all over the United States."[58] In Guilford, Connecticut, Bob Hemstock staked his case against the power company on the reports of scientific studies he had found in local libraries. At Woburn, Massachusetts, where the drinking water was contaminated with chemical solvents and many children had leukemia, residents formed an alliance with faculty at the Harvard School of Public Health to collect information to dispute the finding that no link existed between the water and the leukemias.[59] In Michigan during a protest over contaminated cattle feed, citizens drew on the expertise of a local veterinarian, a private testing laboratory, the National Animal Disease Laboratory, and a USDA research laboratory to counter the Farm Bureau Services' denial that a public problem existed.[60] After the accident at Three Mile Island, a physics professor from the University of California at Berkeley helped nearby residents challenge the Department of Energy's contention that no one had been harmed.[61] At Yellow Creek, Kentucky, a physician and a psychologist helped people fighting against water pollution to do a community health survey that linked the pollution with disease rates.[62] In Ann Arbor, Michigan, a group challenging an industry's plan to discharge contaminated water into a local stream got aid from a chemist, an industrial engineer, a hydrologist, and a former member of a National Academy of Sciences committee.[63] In Flint, Michigan, residents protesting the state's decision to allow a hazardous waste incinerator in their neighborhood were helped by a toxicologist at the University of Michigan School of Public Health.[64]

A fifth piece of evidence comes from a study specifically testing the idea that citizens reason differently from experts. Jeanne Jabanoski analyzed what she calls the "knowledge" used by the citizen members of a scientific advisory board that was overseeing a lead-mediation project in Toronto. She argues that the citizens, who represented an experienced neighborhood group, were basically no different from the professionals. They used three kinds of knowledge: technical knowledge (knowledge about legal and regulatory, scientific and engineering issues), procedural knowledge (knowledge that facilitated the board's decision-making process), and observational knowledge (knowledge of local conditions and history).[65]

By listing these pieces of evidence that members of grassroots groups often use scientific reasoning to understand pollution, I do not mean that they all use it rigorously. Anyone who has spoken with more than a few grassroots activists, or who has been one, or who has attended public meetings where members of community groups testify has heard some activists who sound exceptionally well informed about toxicology and epidemiology and others who seem to have a weak grasp on even basic scientific concepts. Nor do I mean that members of grassroots groups limit themselves to scientific reasoning. On the contrary, their written and oral statements typically combine research data with passionate outrage. Most important, I do not mean that by using science, grassroots groups level the playing field. Industries producing pollution have many more resources to generate and disseminate scientific information than do communities exposed to the pollution. Nevertheless, the available record suggests that (1) when local activists seek advice from political organizers on how to win, they are told to arm themselves with science, and (2) they frequently take the advice.

The available record is, of course, both incomplete and mixed. As I will show in the next chapter, members of grassroots groups often brush off the very idea that they should invite scientists to the table. But it is a mistake to think that citizens in grassroots groups who see the pollution in their neighborhood as risky use a form of reasoning different from that used by professionals. More accurately, it is professionals who tell them what is risky. On one level these professionals are the men and women who write or publicly support reports like *Intolerable Risk*, which serve as agenda setters for public policy making. On another level these professionals are the men and women who work with grassroots groups to find data that link the pollution in their specific areas with adverse health outcomes. If members of a grassroots group take positions about environmental risk that differ from the EPA's or the state health department's, they are probably not using different forms of reasoning. More likely, they are consulting different, more environmentalist, scientists.

I have been arguing that the risk literature misunderstands the conflict over the dangers of environmental pollution because it ignores the citizens' organizations through which people participate in government. It thus treats protesting citizens as isolated individuals, motivated by their untutored, personal perceptions about technology. In taking this position the risk literature disregards the campaigns by national environmental groups that disseminate scientific information about pollution to the general public and overlooks the use by grassroots environmental groups of locally available scientific expertise. My underlying point has been that conflicts over the dangers of environmental pollution are conflicts among scientists, not conflicts between scientists and laypeople.

Because it misconstrues the conflict, the risk literature provides government agencies with a poor solution. Its risk communication guidelines insult the members of grassroots groups by treating them either as primitives who need edification or as exotics who use quaint reasoning. Beyond that, the guidelines are not useful to governments. Some guidelines try to have it both ways, telling agency personnel to simultaneously respect citizens' ideas about what is dangerous and to change them. Other guidelines merely describe a process, advocating two-way communication but failing to face the fact that the two communicating parties typically have opposed policy objectives.

The risk communication guidelines *are* based on an important principle. They recognize that "risk" has many dimensions and that the general public's view of risk is usually broader and richer than the experts'. But in most conflicts over the safety of exposure to environmental pollution, government agencies are not dealing with the general public. They are dealing with members of organized citizens' groups who reason much as experts do. These groups do not protest pollution because it is unobservable, unfamiliar, uncontrollable, or inequitably distributed. They protest because pollution may cause health problems. If, in addition, it has properties that make it "unknown" and "dread," people have all the more reason to oppose it. But the basic logic grassroots groups use is scientific. Thus, the problem for health and environment agencies is not how to handle angry people and it is not how to convince people to stop protesting. The problem is how to make policies when reputable scientists disagree about the dangers of environmental pollution.

Environmental policy making, however, is not always based on science. Moreover, despite the picture I have drawn in this chapter, citizens' groups do not always use science in their struggle with environmental policy makers. In the next chapter I consider some of the drawbacks for grassroots groups in using scientific reasoning. I show that these groups also use commonsense reasoning, both as a deliberate political strategy and as an apparently intuitive reaction to pollution. And I discuss the source of the common sense.

6 | Experiential Knowledge

In Chapter Five I argue—in contrast to the risk literature—that members of grassroots groups who fight
against exposure to environmental pollution base their struggle on the
presumed health effects of pollution not on its perceived social attributes. One way to think about this use of scientific rationality is to consider it to be a political strategy. Elsewhere, Bruce Williams and I have
called the strategy "disinterested politics."[1] In disinterested politics, citizens present their claims as though the claims were free from selfish interests or personal investment. All that counts, they say (or imply), are
the facts, established by objective scientific research and presented
without bias.

The strategy has a long history. Since at least the nineteenth century,
politically disadvantaged groups have used disinterested politics to
argue for social equality. For example, Frederick Douglass, who primarily depended on moral reasoning to fight slavery, also employed science. In an 1854 address, he attacked the craniology research that
showed blacks to be inherently inferior to whites. After explaining the
studies' weaknesses, he adopted the same conceptual categories to
demonstrate that blacks and whites have more anatomical similarities
than differences. From there he argued that, since the two races are in
the same human family, blacks could not be denied full citizenship on
scientific grounds.[2] Similarly, nineteenth-century feminists, whose opposition to the status of women was largely couched in ethical terms, also
used scientific argumentation. One example is Charlotte Perkins
Gilman, who drew on Darwin to promote the feminist cause. She argued
that the subjugation of women violated the law of evolution and that the

whole human species was disadvantaged by the social inequality between the sexes.[3]

Disinterested politics can be a formidable strategy because it does not seem to be about political matters. Instead of raising fractious questions about the distribution of power, about justice, democracy, or fairness, its practioners stick to empirical research. They say to legislators or bureaucrats, "Look, here are the results of the scientific investigations on this subject. These are the facts. If you pass laws or sanction practices that ignore the facts, you will be unmasked as an ideologue or as a pawn of special interests." Of course, from the social constructionist perspective I lay out in Chapter Three, the claim to be presenting simple, objective facts is naive. Science always occurs in a cultural context; its conceptual categories, its rules of evidence, its distinction between appropriate and inappropriate subjects for investigation all reflect the society within which scientists work. But constructionism has never made a big splash in government. Legislators and regulators have little use for meta-analyses. For them, science is the means to *avoid* bias in public policies. Pressure groups who present well-documented scientific studies, published in prestigious professional journals, help policy makers present themselves as dealers in the truth.

Powerful as disinterested politics can be, however, it is also a risky strategy, especially for environmental health activists. One problem is that you have to put all your eggs in one fragile basket. Although the spread of environmentalist thought has affected the kinds of questions environmental scientists ask, with the result that increasing numbers of studies corroborate environmentalists' claims, the environmentalist case is still assailable. As we have seen, robust data showing that exposure to chemicals harms human health are hard to generate, and even when such data exist, they can usually be challenged by other studies.

A second problem with disinterested politics is that it hands over control of the political struggle to outsiders. The scientific community becomes the arbitrator of the validity of the activists' claims. The people who struggled to call attention to environmental pollution are left holding an empty bag if "gatekeepers" such as toxicologists, geologists, and epidemiologists announce that the pollution is innocuous.[4]

The third problem is that disinterested politics limits the roles available to ordinary movement activists. As long as the issue is defined as scientific, people without technical expertise have nothing pertinent to say to policy makers. Most activists are relegated to a kind of Greek chorus. They can comment on the proceedings, but they cannot participate.

Given the problems with using disinterested politics, it is not surprising that many grassroots activists turn to another strategy to keep environmental toxins out of their neighborhood. Instead of grounding demands on erudite, scientific knowledge, they ground demands on the experiential knowledge of ordinary people living in polluted communities. They talk about common sense; they talk about intuition; they talk about what is "obvious" to anyone living their lives. The strategy is a variation on the identity politics common in movements for social equality.

In this chapter I describe identity politics and its use in other social movements. I give examples of its employment by grassroots activists fighting pollution, and, in particular, I demonstrate the intensity of the activists' conviction that the experience of living in polluted neighborhoods gives them special insights into the health effects of environmental pollution. As I write, I keep in mind the lessons from Chapter Two: the relationship between industrial chemicals and disease is not something one can just observe, as one can see that fire burns people or that falling from a great height breaks bones. It is not something one can learn by consulting one's body, as is the realization that if you do not eat dinner you will be really hungry by bedtime or that if you run very fast you will get out of breath. In order to know that an environmental pollutant could cause a health problem, or to know that a cluster of environmental diseases exists in your neighborhood, you, or somebody, has to carry out complex toxicological and epidemiological investigations.

I argue at the end of this chapter that what activists take to be their experiential knowledge about environmental toxins does not come directly from their personal experience but is filtered through the teachings of the environmental movement. I discuss in Chapter Three the data showing that the environmental movement has influenced people's beliefs about nature. My point here is that the movement has also influenced people's beliefs about disease causality.

Identity Politics

Academic writing on identity politics concentrates on struggles for social equality: the civil rights movement, the women's movement, the gay and lesbian movement, the disability movement. In all these campaigns, disparaged or ignored people work to replace negative stereotypes with strong and positive images of themselves. Although much of what scholars call identity politics is the complicated process by which people replace the negative concepts they had of themselves with positive ones, identity politics is also about the struggle to change the general public's preconceptions about denigrated populations.[5] In this process, people who have come to share an identity argue to policy makers and to the general public that the conventional wisdom about who they are was concocted by outsiders. They say that the real truth about blacks or Latinos or women or gays or disabled people can best be known by, and imparted by, the people who actually embody those identities.

James Baldwin was practicing identity politics in 1955 when he published *Notes of a Native Son*, a book that bolstered the civil rights movement and that told white people what it was like to be black in America. Middle-class white women in consciousness-raising groups were doing identity politics in the late 1960s and early 1970s when they asked, "What do we know about ourselves, from our own experience, that differs from what men say about us?"[6] During the same period, black women raising their children on welfare were doing identity politics when they formed the National Welfare Rights Organization and insisted that their own perspectives on living in poverty should guide welfare policy.[7] In the late 1970s and the 1980s, as international human rights became a political issue, Rigoberta Menchu in Guatemala and Domitila Barrios de Chungara in Bolivia practiced identity politics in their own countries and aboard as they traveled from forum to forum describing to outsiders what life was like for indigenous peoples in Latin America.[8] Most recently, disability rights activists in the United States have done much the same thing, arguing that injury-prevention campaigns stigmatize people with disabilities.[9] The message these men and women deliver is this: We are the ones who know; we are the authorities on our lives; you who do not live in our circumstances can never fully understand. But listen to us carefully. We who actually experience bigotry and prejudice will tell you what to do to bring about justice.

The environmental movement initially had little room for identity politics because in the late 1960s and early 1970s the movement was not primarily about the harm one group of people had inflicted on another. It was about the harm human beings have inflicted on nature. Environmentalists argued that we humans are all in this together. We have hurt nature by our actions, and now we have a collective responsibility to protect the animals and plants, the mountains and lakes and oceans with which we share the planet. Unlike movements for social equality, environmentalism began as an inclusive struggle. No race, gender, or class owned the movement; no group claimed to have a perspective better than any other group of citizens.

Then things shifted. In the late 1970s, communities exposed to industrial wastes and pesticides redefined the environmental problem. For them, the issue was not the responsibility humans have to protect nature but the responsibility governments and industries have to protect citizens against toxic substances. The victims were not endangered species and tropical forests but specific women and men and children in particular neighborhoods whose health had been or could be affected by exposure to pollution.[10]

This change in problem definition provided a space within environmentalism for the identity politics used in movements for social equality. The new activists said that not all people are in this together. They argued, and they continue to argue, that people exposed to pollution are in a different situation from the rest of the population and that their personal experiences as victims give them a clearer understanding of the issues. They say that the elites who make, or influence, environmental policies—government leaders, businesspeople, scientists, and mainstream environmentalists with offices in Washington, D.C.—are too personally disengaged from the problem to comprehend it well. Wisdom lies with the experiential knowledge of the people who contend with polluted water, soil, or air in their everyday lives.

In contrasting identity politics with disinterested politics, I do not mean that the identity politics used by grassroots toxics groups is antiscience. On the contrary, as we have seen, members of these groups place great faith in science. Over and over they say, both explicitly and implicitly, that science is the route to truth. They are not relativists, believing in the existence of many truths; nor are they mystics, putting more store in spiritual wisdom than in scientific investigations. Their position is that good science—science done by honest and objective investigators—reveals the truth that environmental pollution causes many of their health problems. If, in some cases, no evidence exists for such a conclusion, it is because honest and objective studies have not yet been done. By the same token, if some studies show that a community's exposure to pollution is safe, it is because the researchers were dishonest or biased.

The difference between disinterested politics and identity politics is that in disinterested politics, scientific evidence is the centerpiece of the political argument. People trying to influence government or public opinion act as though they take seriously the possibility that exposure might be safe, and they present scientific evidence that exposure is, in fact, harmful. In identity politics, science stays in the background. People trying to influence government or public opinion act as though science has already proved indubitably that exposure poses a serious public health hazard. The centerpiece of their argument is the corroborating knowledge they get from their personal experiences.[11]

Identity Poltics in Action

The Center for Health, Environment and Justice (CHEJ), the predominant support group for toxics activists, has probably done more than any other organization to encourage activists to use identity politics.[12] Keenly aware that bringing science to the table can turn a community's fight against pollution into a tedious standoff between "dueling experts," CHEJ warns against disinterested politics. "Experts can't solve your problems," CHEJ's science director tells activists. "[N]o one knows more about a community and its situation than the people directly affected.... Trust your instincts; rarely will you go wrong if you follow what you know in your heart to be true and right."[13] Even though CHEJ has produced a handbook telling grassroots groups how to find and use experts, the organization advises activists to draw on their personal experiences. The handbook urges readers to "keep in mind that your own community expertise is a powerful weapon to use when your opponents roll out their experts. For example, if you live in a farm community, isn't it common sense that people who've worked the land all their lives will have opinions about the ground that are at least as valid as some 'hired gun' expert from some far-away university?"[14]

The instincts, the opinions, the heartfelt knowledge that CHEJ encourages people to consult come down to a crystalline understanding that when a community is polluted and people living there have many diseases, the pollution caused the diseases. The understanding is not ideological. The people CHEJ addresses rarely consider themselves environmentalists—at least not when they first organize into protest groups. But they have seen the children with birth defects; they have heard their neighbors talk heartbrokenly about miscarriages; they have driven their friends to chemotherapy appointments. At the same time, they have observed the industry smokestacks and the waste treatment plants. The connection is simple common sense. As a member of the South Bronx Clean Air Coalition said:

> Our community has one of the highest rates of infant mortality, persons with compromised immune systems, lead poisoning, and asthma. But this comes as no surprise, because in our immediate community there are over 65 waste transfer stations transporting asbestos, lead piping, construction debris, medical waste, sludge and many other toxins to places all over the U.S.[15]

In another community an activist made the same point, putting it in a less cynical, more pugnacious way:

> I did not come to the fight against environmental problems as an intellectual but rather as a concerned mother.... People say, "But you're not a scientist. How do you know it's not safe?"... I have common sense.... I know if dioxin and mercury are going to come out of an incinerator stack, somebody's going to be affected.[16]

To grassroots activists the insight about pollution that seems to spring from their daily existence is much like the knowledge African Americans have about the existence of racism or the cognizance gays have about homophobia. In such cases, people say that the reality of the situation is obvious to anyone experiencing it. "If you walked in our shoes," they tell doubters, "you would understand how deep the prejudice is in our society." Like people struggling for social equality, toxics activists are indignant when policy makers act as though their situation has to be uncovered and certified by professional experts. To those experiencing life with pollution, nothing about it is obscure. In the words of one woman: "Once you've had someone in your family who has been attacked by the environment—I mean who has had cancer or other disease—you get a keen sense of what is going on."[17] Another woman said, when the Centers for Disease Control found her community's health data statistically nonsignificant, "Statistics don't tell you. People do. I've walked this creek and I've seen the sick people."[18]

Lois Gibbs, the Love Canal leader, made the same point when the New York Department of Health finally announced, in 1997, that it would conduct a comprehensive health survey of former Love Canal residents. A health department spokeswoman had justified the survey by explaining, "If we can tell residents they are at higher statistical risk, they can inform their physicians, which hopefully will lead to early diagnosis." Gibbs's scornful response: "Does this woman think the residents who were surrounded by chemicals and watched their neighbors get sick... don't already know they are at high risk?"[19]

It's difficult to exaggerate the firmness of this experiential knowledge. Whereas environmental health scientists tend to speak about their knowledge tentatively, grassroots activists do not. The evidence of their own experience is simply unmistakable. Consider the man living in polluted Hardeman County, Tennessee, who told a reporter he knew the company (Velsicol) was dumping toxic material:

> But I never thought it'd get in our water. I'd take a bath and break out, like chickenpox. Take another bath and there's the pox again. I took a water sample to the health department; they said nothing's wrong with it. I thought they was good people, smarter than I was. But they wasn't.[20]

Or take the example of a woman whose neighborhood in Anniston, Alabama, is contaminated with PCBs from a Monsanto plant. "My daughter played in that ditch," she said, speaking of a channel that for years carried chemical waste from the plant, "and my grandbabies, both of them, live on breathing machines.... My oldest son played in that ditch. His baby doesn't have any joints in her fingers.... It all comes from the chemicals. We lived in it all our lives, and this is the result."[21]

A long-term environmental activist in southwestern Detroit is similarly sure of the relation between chemical exposure and disease. In an interview with me, she said that, for people in her community, environmental health was "the scariest thing." She continued, "People are afraid to think about it, afraid to know the full consequences of exposure.... There are lots of cancer clusters, clusters of very rare kinds of cancer."

"But why do people think the environment has caused the clusters?" I asked.

"Well, it's obvious."

"Why is it obvious?" I pressed.

"The air has all this stuff in it. The water is full of junk, the food is full of stuff. The chemicals are everywhere."[22]

The clarity of this knowledge goes a long way toward explaining the pugnacity of toxics groups. When people living in polluted areas come face to face with government bureaucrats who tell them they are not in danger, they become enraged. It is not just the government position itself that angers them but the epistemological source of the position.

Government officials say that as long as the industry in question operates in accordance with environmental laws and regulations, the chemical waste it puts out is by definition harmless to public health. Official knowledge is thus abstract, general, and static. The community's knowledge is concrete, specific, and dynamic. In residents' minds, it springs from the actual sights, smells, and tastes, the tactile and emotional experiences they encounter in their everyday lives.

For many people, the government's challenge to the authenticity of their experience is a major spur to activism. After a meeting in Albuquerque with representatives from a variety of government agencies, one community member reported:

> I didn't want to say much.... I'm not well educated. I can't speak the way they do. But when they got to talking, they were wrong at what they were saying. I knew I was right. So I just got up and said, "Wait a minute!" And since then I am not afraid of anybody. I live here. I know what is going on.[23]

In south-central Los Angeles, women fighting against operation of an incinerator were similarly angered when officials told them they were not at risk. In this case, officials implied that something residents knew from their experience to be perfectly safe was actually harmful. In the words of one observer, "[E]xpert assurance that health risks associated with dioxin exposure were less than those associated with 'eating peanut butter' unleashed a fury of dissent. All the women, young and old, working-class and professional, had made peanut butter sandwiches for years."[24]

The customary settings where grassroots activists express their knowledge are local hearings in which environmental agencies take public testimony before deciding whether to issue permits to industries. The hearings tend to be brief and focused on the narrow issues covered by the permit—a situation that limits people's opportunity to talk about their personal experiences with pollution. But an unusual three-day conference in February 1994 gave activists a wide-open arena in which to do identity politics. It provides a dramatic instance of the strategy in action. The conference, held in Arlington, Virginia, and sponsored by seven federal agencies, attracted some one thousand people; about half were federal policy makers and half were grassroots leaders from around the country.[25] It was prompted by the data on "environmental racism," which have demonstrated that people of color and poor people are more likely than others to live near hazardous waste sites.[26]

A major conference theme was the importance of community participation in government decision making at polluted, or potentially polluted, sites. Yet, at the end of the first day, attendees told conference leaders that there was not enough community participation at the conference itself. As a result, three plenary session speakers—EPA chief Carol Browner, David Satcher, who was then head of the ATSDR, and Thomas Gumbly, an administrator at the Department of Energy—gave only brief remarks and then asked for comments from the audience. Dozens of angry community activists lined up behind the microphones to speak. The published proceedings of the symposium fail to capture the emotional intensity of these long sessions, but they do transmit the activists' clear message: Government officials do not understand the problem; it is the *community* that has the definitive wisdom about exposure to environmental pollution.

The message was most dramatically expressed by the many Native Americans in attendance who argued at several points during the conference that Native Americans have a special kind of knowledge garnered from generations of close interaction with nature. But the message also came from a whole variety of Americans. To the encouraging applause and sympathetic murmurs of other activists, people described their experiences of living with hazardous waste landfills and incinerators, poisoned drinking water, contaminated air, toxic soil, deep-injection wells, radioactive waste, and pesticide exposure. They told the government representatives about deaths and diseases in their communities, and they reported that federal and state bureaucrats failed to see what was plain to anyone living in these communities: the diseases and deaths were caused by the hazards. Here are a few examples:

A man from Yellow Creek, Kentucky, told about the death of a fifteen-year-old girl who had been poisoned by drinking water. He said the community knew that a local tanning company poisoned the water, a tanning company licensed by the EPA. A man from East St. Louis reported that twenty-five people on one block near a chemical company had died of cancer during a five-year period, and 45 percent of the families have one or more members with cancer, yet the EPA refuses to see the obvious connection to the chemical company. A woman in Winona, Texas, said she knew that people in her community were suffering and dying because of chemical injection wells, but the EPA acted as though this were not the case. A woman from Howell County in Georgia described an area in her town where sixteen factories dump waste and where twenty people on one street have died. She said the EPA has found toxic materials in the soil but fails to recognize the link between the toxins and the deaths.[27]

Several scientists at the conference also argued that the community can see things that more-removed people cannot. Among them was David Ozonoff, an epidemiologist at the Boston University School of Public Health. Ozonoff said that the environmental health "research agenda must be informed and derived from collaboration with the affected communities." He suggested that there are "useful ways to classify environmental burdens that express how they are experienced by the affected communities" and that such classifications might "reveal effects that are not visible when more academically conventional categories are used."[28] Linda Rae Murray, the physician who directs Winfield Moody Health Center in Chicago, also called for citizens' ideas. She emphasized not just the experiential knowledge available to *any* person exposed to pollution but also the knowledge minorities have. "Across the country, minority factory workers can tell scientists and government agencies how toxic chemicals get into the body, what to do about it, and why contaminating practices should stop."[29]

Problems and Promises in Using Identity Politics

Similar to using disinterested politics, using identity politics in environmental health disputes has some real disadvantages. First, and most obvious, it does not always work. Policy makers may listen respectfully to people's statements about the health effects of exposure to pollution but still maintain that the agency cannot act to protect a community's health without scientific evidence that the pollution has harmed, or could harm, the population living there. No matter how forcefully people argue that anyone with common sense can see that they are in danger, government agencies can justify inaction by continuing to ask for "the facts." In other words, agencies can refuse to play identity politics, insisting that the only legitimate game is disinterested politics. Science is still the most prestigious form of knowledge in modern societies, and in the health field public policies not justified by scientific findings are easily ridiculed. As an EPA scientist said at the Arlington conference, "The credibility of [our agency's] decisions depends on science, and better data is needed to identify risk."[30] The fact that grassroots activists using identity politics are convinced that good science supports their

knowledge (or would support their knowledge were the research conducted) does not lessen the agency's political need to actually have the
research in hand.

A second disadvantage of practicing identity politics is that, because
its topic is whatever feelings people find in their hearts, community
groups can be publicly embarrassed by their supporters' declarations. In
Arlington, possibly only a few attendees were discomfited by the testimony of the woman who reported that people became sick at her workplace when they were given aspirin that had "expired 6 or 7 years earlier." People at the conference might have been unaware that the only
thing wrong with expired aspirin is its possible loss of potency. But there
was plenty of squirming when Dick Gregory (once a popular comedian,
now a political activist) presented, apparently in full seriousness, his explanation for violence in black communities. He was responding to a
lunchtime address on the importance of establishing good relations between university scientists and communities. Gregory said that "science"
causes the violence. People are shot in order to provide cadavers for
medical research, since seatbelt laws have decreased the number available. The proof is that most victims are shot in the head so their internal
organs will not be damaged. The aspirin woman and Dick Gregory both
said that they knew well what they were talking about because the events
happened in their own communities.[31]

In addition to being publicly embarrassed by their supporters'
naiveté about medications or their grandiose theorizing, community
groups practicing identity politics can be embarrassed by their supporters' politics. The genuine voice of the community, expressing what
people know in their hearts, can be racist, sexist, and homophobic. Consider the white construction worker who told Studs Turkel that he knows
from experience that the worst stereotypes of African Americans are cor-
rect: "I seen 'em. They live like low-lifes. Don't like to work. Let their
homes run down."[32] Or think of the folks whose common sense told
them that school children with the AIDS virus threaten other kids'
health.[33]

A third disadvantage in practicing identity politics is that community
groups' claims can be undercut by neighbors who also speak from personal experience but whose experience is different. At Love Canal, a
third of the residents felt no connection between the status of their
health and exposure to the hazardous waste. They lived in exactly the
same neighborhood and had seen and smelled the same polluted area

around the old waste dump as the members of the Love Canal Homeowners Association, yet they insisted that in their experience, no health
effects had occurred. Thus they opposed the association's whole campaign. As Martha Fowlkes and Patricia Miller say, these residents were
"implicitly allied with official science."[34]

The fact that anyone can practice identity politics, however, is also
one of its strengths and a reason political organizers promote it. The
success of a social movement organization depends partly on its ability
to recruit members. If members have not much to do beyond attending
meetings, they may well drop out. But if they can speak their minds in
public hearings or talk directly to legislators they are likely to feel both
personally efficacious (which is often one goal of political organizers)
and essential to the success of the organization.[35] Moreover, if what they
have on their minds is a crystal clear understanding drawn from their
own personal experience, they are not apt to be intimidated by opponents who have only secondary information.

Identity politics can also draw favorable media attention, thus promoting the movement to the public at large—a less probable outcome
of using disinterested politics. "Nothing is more powerful than people
who live at the site speaking out for themselves," says the Center for
Health, Environment and Justice. "Ask yourselves, who's more impressive: Mrs. Dee Oxin who'll talk about the miscarriages she's suffered
from exposure, or your expert, Mr. A. Thority, who'll describe laboratory studies on toxicity? Who's going to motivate the audience? Who's
going to be on the 10 o'clock news?"[36]

A third reason to practice identity politics is that it is supported by a
venerable epistemological theory. The theory posits that victims of injustice or oppression have a privileged vantage point for understanding the
world. Its political implication is that the reports of such people should
have greater weight with policy makers than reports by elites. The theory
is important enough to deserve its own section in this chapter. I introduce it below and then argue that, despite the theoretical support it
gives identity politics, it misdirects scholarly analyses of grassroots
groups' fight against exposure to pollution.

Experiential Knowledge and Social Status

The idea that social status explains knowledge goes back at least to
Marx. From a Marxist perspective, people's understanding of reality is

linked to the work they do. Put simply, people who work on the assembly line develop a kind of knowledge different from the knowledge acquired by people who own and sell the products coming off that line. The workers' knowledge is not simply technical knowledge about how to make the product, nor is the owners' knowledge merely about how to market it. Each group, because of its relation to the means of production, develops a distinct understanding about society, a different kind of consciousness, a particular set of concepts and values. These two perspectives are not equally valid. The owners of the means of production have a partial and thus inaccurate view of reality; the workers' understanding is more complete and more reliable.

Why should the workers' knowledge be more complete? The reason, ironically, is that the owners' knowledge usually predominates. Marx, seeing society divided into the ruling class and the proletariat, said that the ruling class gains so much political power that it governs even the consciousness of the proletariat. In his famous words from *The German Ideology:* "The ideas of the ruling class are in every epoch the ruling ideas."[37] More recent scholars, notably Raymond Williams, argue that the domination is never total. The subjugated class also has the consciousness gained from its fundamental relation to production. Thus, whereas the owners of production have only one kind of knowledge, workers end up with two. One is the knowledge they get from the institutions dominated by the ruling class—the schools, the media, the government. The other is the knowledge they acquire from their own daily activities in the production process. Drawing on the first kind of knowledge, people see the present structure of society as serving everyone well. Drawing on the second kind of knowledge, people see the structure as mainly benefiting the dominant class. The political struggle for workers is to nurture and spread their experiential knowledge about society in the face of the opposing and more culturally powerful knowledge owners have and promote.[38]

In recent years, a group of feminist scholars has added a new dimension to this analysis. They argue that the most fundamental division in society is not between the ruling class and the proletariat but between men and women. The worker Marx had in mind, says Nancy Hartsock, is indeed immersed in a worker's world while on the job. But when he goes home, he is no longer subjugated: "He who followed behind as the worker, timid and holding back, with nothing to expect but a hiding, now strides in front, while a third person, not specifically present in

Marx's account of the transactions between capitalist and worker (both of whom are male) follows timidly behind, carrying groceries, baby, and diapers." Hartsock argues that because women are constantly in the subjugated position, "the vision of reality which grows from the female experience is deeper and more thoroughgoing than that available to the worker."[39] From their unique perspective—Hartsock calls it the feminist standpoint—women can more truly comprehend our male-dominated culture.[40]

Sandra Harding offers a similar analysis. Women have a clearer understanding of the world they live in, she says, because they are perpetual outsiders. The social structure was not designed for women and it does not fit with their experiences. In order to negotiate successfully within the structure, women must constantly analyze it. They are like people living in a foreign country where many aspects of everyday life seem slightly peculiar, not what one would intuitively expect. For men, on the other hand, the social structure feels natural. Regardless of their relation to the means of production, they cannot easily see the structure's workings because society was designed by men and for men's needs. Their experiences and society are in harmony.[41]

In both its original and its feminist version, this epistemological theory moves identity politics from the utilitarian realm to the realm of moral imperatives. It means that marginalized people who demand new laws, regulations, and policies are not just exercising their democratic rights; they are speaking truth to power. It should be no wonder that the theory underlies all the statements about knowledge by grassroots groups and grassroots support groups or that it is implied in much of the academic literature on grassroots activism.

The theory, however, creates an intellectual dilemma in three parts. First, it provides few avenues for impugning whatever racist, sexist, homophobic, or simply naive views nonelites might hold—a predicament I touch on earlier in this chapter. Second, it can lead to exactly the sort of essentialism that progressive politics seeks to overcome. Because it contends that true knowledge comes directly from the raw experiences of marginalized folk, it fits with the belief that particular classes or races or genders have an inherent, fixed "essence." It thus implies that differences among social groups are inborn biological traits, an implication that risks naturalizing, and thus justifying, unequal treatment.[42] And third—the problem I am most concerned with here—it depicts a type of knowledge that is static and inflexible. The theory cannot account for the fluidity of knowledge and ideas. Particularly, it cannot explain why marginalized people today have special knowledge about environmental pollution when they had no such knowledge earlier. As I note in Chapter Three, mothers used to watch benignly as their children ran behind the trucks that sprayed DDT around the neighborhood. In contrast to the people I quote in this chapter, women then apparently had no deep-seated intuition that the chemical compound was dangerous. Nor did they have a commonsense understanding that the smoke from industrial stacks or the waste chemicals dumped in the ground and discharged into local streams and ponds—so much more rampant then—caused disease. And even though many more people had chronic diseases such as cancer, we have no record of a common intuition that synthetic chemicals were the cause.[43]

What *can* explain the new knowledge is the development and widespread promotion of environmentalism. Environmentalist principles negate the old common sense about nature, transforming nature from something tough into something fragile. Now embraced by people throughout society, the principles make it obvious that releasing synthetic substances into the air, water, and soil is apt to be dangerous. And they lend themselves easily to a cognizance that human beings who encounter those substances are also at risk. In other words, what grassroots activists see as their experiential knowledge about the effects of industrial pollution, and what some theorists would explain as a consequence of their marginal social status, comes neither directly from personal experience nor from social status. The knowledge is filtered through the teachings of the environmental movement.

Explaining Experiential Knowledge

Environmentalists have fostered their new principles through a variety of avenues. Often, the promotion of environmentalism is very subtle. The passages I quote earlier from CHEJ publications advising grassroots activists to use their common sense about pollution can all be read as just that: advice. At the same time, however, much of what CHEJ writes can be construed as an environmental education campaign. Embedded in its counsel to activists are the messages that nonnatural chemicals are dangerous, that even natural substances are dangerous if they become part of industrial production, and that, in general, human interference in nature is extremely risky. In other words, CHEJ both urges grassroots activists to use their common sense and teaches them what common sense is. In the passage I quoted about Mr. A. Thority and Mrs. Dee Oxin, it is common sense that exposure to pollution caused Mrs. Oxin's miscarriages. CHEJ does not defend this attribution of causality as though it were controversial; the organization simply takes it for granted. Readers are expected to do the same. More important, so are viewers of the 10 o'clock news.

The other statements in this chapter by people fighting pollution (except the one from my own interview that has not been published before) are also part of environmental education. They come from publications intended for the general population and from a public conference. Each statement provides readers (or listeners) with an environmentalist interpretation of their own experiences, an interpretation that is all the more powerful for not calling attention to itself. The environmentalism I describe in Chapter Three is *assumed* in these statements. The speakers are not consciously doing environmental education to persuade people that nature is exquisitely interrelated and likely to be harmed by human interference. As many scholars have noted, toxics activists, both in grassroots groups and in grassroots support groups, typically do not think of themselves as environmentalists. Indeed, some take pains to distinguish themselves from environmentalists.[44] Yet, what they say about chemicals and health follows and underscores the messages that writers like Rachel Carson began sending out in the 1960s and that mainstream organizations like NRDC have been delivering since the 1970s.

In that sense they are like any number of Americans who do not think of themselves as particularly political but whose opinions replicate the classical liberalism developed and promoted by political philosophers as Europe became industrialized. Both the people who have absorbed environmentalism and the people who have absorbed classical liberalism pass on to others these forms of understanding the world. And they do so in an extraordinarily powerful way. They do not present an explicit philosophy, hold it up for examination in contrast to other philosophies, and then argue that the philosophy should guide one's actions. Instead, they presuppose the philosophy. They take it as a statement of fact about the world, believe that those who do not act in its light are ideologues, and argue that truth should guide one's actions.

By using this analogy, I do not mean to imply that classical liberalism and environmentalism have the same kind of political implications.

Clearly, environmentalism today has the potential to justify more-progressive social change than does nineteenth-century liberalism. My point is that, in relation to environmentalist ideas, members of grassroots groups are both passive and active. On the one hand, they have assimilated environmentalist ideas about nature and thus have available within themselves a new interpretation of their experiences. On the other hand, they transmit environmentalist teachings in the very act of demanding environmental changes as a means to prevent disease.

At this point, the reader might contend that people's new intuition about chemicals has little to do with environmentalism. Maybe people now know that their exposure to pollution is dangerous simply because scientists have told them so. I come close to suggesting that situation myself in Chapter Five when I argue that grassroots groups use scientific reasoning in their fight against exposure to pollution. Certainly it is true that scientific knowledge about environmental pollutants has increased greatly in the last thirty years. And historically, people's intuition about disease has often changed in response to scientific discoveries. In the early nineteenth century, most physicians believed that the major epidemic diseases were caused by the odor of decaying organic matter. The general public thought so too. It seemed entirely reasonable. Disease and death rates were lower in rural areas than in the urban slums, where a disgusting stench continuously rose up from piles of rotting kitchen wastes dumped in the streets, from overflowing outhouses behind the buildings, and from animal excrement. Everybody avoided smells to the extent they could; you only needed common sense to know they caused disease. Later in the century, physicians learned that the smells themselves were not dangerous; the major diseases were caused by microorganisms. Public health officials began spreading this new message to the public. After hearing it over and over, people eventually acquired a new common sense. They no longer worried about miasmas but about germs. Today it is common knowledge that unwashed hands and bodies as well as imperfectly scrubbed dishes and cooking utensils—however clean they may look and smell—can harbor disease-causing bacteria and viruses. We are not only taught this specifically by every authoritative voice; it seems intuitively true.[45]

However, the suggestion that people assume that their exposure to pollution is dangerous because scientists have said so ignores what is going on in the world. It pretends that scientists agree on the health effects of pollution. It presumes the existence of a scientific consensus on synthetic chemicals as a cause of disease similar to the consensus on germs as a cause of disease. But in a world in which reputable scientists (still) debate the health dangers of pollution, and in which, for most pollutants, clear evidence for either side is hard to find, the appeal to science is disingenuous. If we thought that people's intuition about environmental health came from science, we would need to ask why people are willing to give the benefit of the doubt to scientific studies that support environmentalism instead of to the studies that do not.

When grassroots activists demand that policy makers protect them from exposure to industrial pollutants, they often employ a form of identity politics. They base their demand on their own experience living with pollution, telling policy makers about the terrible effects the exposure has had on their health and the health of their families and neighbors. Regardless of the fact that, in contrast to the causes of conditions such as broken bones and burns, the causes of cancers, birth defects, and infertility are impossible to witness personally, grassroots activists draw on their own common sense to make the causal connection. Grassroots support groups encourage local activists to employ a kind of identity politics, advising them that, because they live every day with pollution and actually witness the health problems in their communities, they have a clearer understanding than the experts about what is dangerous. And the activists agree. The clarity of their knowledge goes a long way toward explaining why they are so shocked and outraged if government agencies do not side with them.

The most influential social theory to address this state of affairs argues that knowledge is related to social class and to gender. Theorists in this field contend that marginalized people have a more complete and thus more accurate understanding of the world than do elites because they are better able to see structures of domination. This epistemological theory is an honorable one in that it provides a reason, besides the simple democratic imperative, for policy makers to listen carefully when such groups as workers or women demand new laws, regulations, and policies. Thus it helps to legitimate a variety of struggles for a more democratic society. Not surprisingly, it is implicit in much of the writing by and about grassroots activists.

The theory, however, fails to explain toxics activism. It cannot account for the long period of time when people living in polluted areas had no experiential or commonsense knowledge about its health effects, and thus had no reason to practice identity politics. To understand why people are protesting against exposure to industrial toxins only now, one has to pay attention to the activities of the environmental movement. The next chapter turns again to that topic.

7 Social Movements and Social Change

I have been painting a picture of the environmental movement as a creator and promoter of new ideas. I have argued that the movement has been so successful at this task that its ideas, once decidedly peculiar, are now becoming simple common sense. They constitute views of the world that both experts and citizens take for granted. Environmental health scientists are now asking new questions, using old methodologies differently, and getting new results. Citizens, for their part, are now embracing new concepts of nature, supporting new kinds of public policies, and adopting new assumptions about disease causality.

This depiction of the environmental movement deviates from most social movement studies in that it focuses on the influence a social movement has on culture. For the most part, social movement scholars theorize in the opposite direction, describing the ways that culture influences movements. They do so because they tend to think of movements in terms of organizations and to ask why organizations form and what makes them successful. In the case of the environmental movement, those organizations are mainstream groups such as the Natural Resources Defense Council, grassroots groups such as Citizens Against Toxic Sprays, and support groups such as the Center for Health, Environment and Justice. In earlier chapters, I, too, pay attention to such groups. And it *is* important to understand how they operate. But the environmental movement, like all social movements, is far larger than the organizations it has spawned. Its "members" are not all in clubs. Indeed, the idea that social movements are composed of members hampers one's ability to see the effects movements have on culture. Unless one includes in the term *social movement* all the movement's actors—the whole gamut of men and women who invent and champion the movement's principles—one is likely to miss a movement's most important contribution. Along with the people who form or join movement organizations, these actors include the writers and scientists I have discussed in this book, as well as a host of journalists, politicians, bureaucrats, educators, artists, and others who use their professional skills to foster the movement. The actors also include large numbers of ordinary people who promote movement principles in their day-to-day lives.

If one pays attention to the actions of all these people, one can see how environmentalists, and indeed the partisans of all other social movements as well, are able to influence culture. In this chapter I locate this culture-creating picture of social movements in the array of literature theorizing about movements. I emphasize particularly the concepts of framing and of hegemony.

Social Movement Theory

Social movement theory since the mid-twentieth century can be divided into two stages. In the first stage, from the 1940s to the 1960s, scholars were concerned primarily with class-based movements such as the labor movement and revolutionary crusades. People studying those phenomena took for granted that collective action by the citizenry is socially destabilizing and usually undesirable. Seeing movements mainly in terms of mobs and violence, most investigators asked how such mobilization can be prevented. Their answers concentrated on the dissatisfactions and malaise of the participants, emphasizing the psychological states of people who rebel, and calling collective action an irrational response to rapid social change. In general, these scholars focused on the individual. They wanted to understand what it was about people's psyches that made them criticize the status quo.[1] Social scientists were not alone in this rather condescending approach. Historians during this era often displayed similar attitudes about the participants in nineteenth-century social movements. They treated abolitionists, for example, as "meddlesome fanatics."[2]

Social movement theory entered into its second, and current, stage in the late 1960s, as large numbers of middle- and upper-middle-class people began taking up the causes of social equality, peace, and environmental protection. A new generation of academics, for whom social movements were suddenly not about "them" but about "us," argued that the old understanding of social movements was too narrow, too negative, and too facile. The old theory, they said, had little room for the movements they saw around them. It made collective action irrational when, in fact, protest is a reasonable, even desirable, response to terrible conditions. And, most erroneously, even when sympathetic to social movements, the old theorists had assumed that protest rises up spontaneously in the face of hardship or injustice, whereas they might better have asked why terrible conditions, which always exist at least to some extent in any society, sometimes generate social movements and sometimes do not.

The new scholarship takes up this question about the generation of social movements, adds to it questions about the successes and failures of movements, and offers three kinds of answers. One answer, which I treat only briefly, concentrates on the mobilization of resources. A second, which I also treat briefly, concentrates on the political opportunity structure. A third answer, the main topic of this chapter, concentrates on values and beliefs.

Scholars in the resource mobilization school primarily study organizational tactics and processes. Within that context, they show that members of social movement organizations need to pay a good deal of attention to the acquisition and employment of resources. It is not enough to have a cause; in order to form and run effective groups, organizations need assets: leaders, money, expertise, and outside support. For example, at least someone in the organization has to know how to use the media, how to run a meeting, how to mobilize new recruits, how to read laws and regulations, and how to talk with policy makers.[3] This approach to social movements has inspired a huge amount of new scholarship, no doubt in part because studying an organization is so much easier than studying something as amorphous as a "movement." My own foray into resource mobilization produced Chapter Five of this book—a chapter that, however little mention it makes of resource mobilization theory, argues that environmental movement organizations need and use scientific expertise.

Scholars studying the political opportunity structure also focus on movement organizations, but they are interested in the characteristics of political regimes that affect the activities and success of movement organizations. Movement actors adopt diverse plans of action and have varied degrees of success depending on whether the political system is composed of relatively open or relatively closed institutions, whether alignments among elites are stable or unstable, whether the state is repressive or liberal, and whether movements have allies among elites.[4] This approach to social movements has particularly inspired comparativists, who have explained the divergent trajectories of the same social movement in different countries as a response to the countries' political structures.[5]

Scholars studying values and beliefs in social movements broaden the scope of inquiry. They acknowledge the importance of resources and political opportunity in understanding movement successes and failures, but they are primarily concerned with the malleability of the normative social codes that shape behavior. They say that a full theory of social movements would reflect the fact that social movement activists, and the people they seek to influence, are embedded in society. Their approach to social movements assumes that people's understanding of reality is socially constructed. In a sense, this way of studying social movements reverts to the pre-1960s theory. But instead of locating beliefs and values in people, it locates them in society.[6]

The most widely cited social movement scholarship in this field revolves about the concept of "framing." The term comes from Erving Goffman, who reasoned that when people recognize a particular event or situation, they are unconsciously applying "interpretive schemata" to what would otherwise be a meaningless jumble. Such schemata, or frames, allow people "to locate, perceive, identify, and label" occurrences and thus to confer some degree of order on the multitude of perceptions that constitute their lives. Goffman was primarily interested in frames that come with, or are a part of, a given culture. As he put it, his work attempts "to isolate some of the basic frameworks of understanding available in our society for making sense out of events."[7] But social movement scholars tend to think of frames in more dynamic terms: they are most interested in the ways that activists in movement organizations manipulate the available cultural frames in order to mobilize people.

As these scholars make clear, all social movement frames are injustice frames. Such frames redefine accepted social conditions as unjust and assign responsibility for that injustice to individuals and institutions other than its victims.[8] In the process of such redefinition, events and experiences that were once culturally unrelated get linked together. The women's movement, for example, placed in a single injustice frame abortion laws, the traditional division of household labor, pornography, and the small number of women in prestigious professions. The environmental movement's injustice frame encompasses such once-disparate occurrences as oil spills, pesticide residues in food, species extinction, and cancer rates.

Nearly all the social movement scholars writing about frames concentrate on the ways in which movement activists *use* them, and particularly on how they use them to mobilize supporters. David Snow and his colleagues have been the most influential of these scholars. In a seminal article on what they call "frame alignment," they argue that a good part of a social movement's success depends on its ability to make movement ideas resonate with what prospective adherents already value and believe.[9] Many other scholars have adopted this reasoning. Sidney Tarrow, for example, says that civil rights activists were able to recruit white liberals to the struggle because they used the venerable American concept of rights to frame their movement.[10] Similarly, Stella Čapek shows how environmental activists mobilized a predominantly black community at a hazardous waste site in Texarkana, Texas, by framing exposure to the site in terms of civil rights.[11] Sheila Foster describes an analogous case in Chester, Pennsylvania.[12]

Other scholars, combining framing and political opportunity approaches, consider the effect of changing political times on social movement framing. For example, Sam Marullo and his colleagues, noting that membership in American peace movement organizations dwindled at the end of the Cold War, show how the remaining activists used mobilization frames that were both broader and more radical than the old frames. Such frames were particularly attractive to people whose long concern with peace had led them to link war to many social factors and to believe in more drastic solutions than had been proposed within the old frames.[13]

Important as this literature has been to understanding the ways that activists deploy frames, however, I have been arguing in this book that social movements do more than simply frame events. Social movement actors create the frames in the first place. If a movement frame gives new meaning to events and experiences, the frame, in a sense, has to *be* that meaning. A social movement frame consists of the principles the movement promotes. And it is in light of these principles that an event or condition can be called unjust. These principles, however, do not exist until people invent them. A social movement frame is not just lying around someplace, available to be picked up and used to focus attention on some hitherto ignored feature of the world, or even to give new meaning to that feature. The frame has to be created.

Social movement framing scholars tend to lose sight of that fact because most of them work on relatively old social movements—those for social equality and for peace—whose movement frames were first constructed in the nineteenth century. Few of the people interested in frames call attention to premovement cultural climates. But before the abolition and feminist movements in the nineteenth century, equality among all people was still a radical, iconoclastic idea; and before the antiwar movement of that era, the principle that nations should settle disputes around the negotiating table was equally strange.[14]

Fortunately for social movement studies, a few scholars writing about today's movements do include sections describing the enormous transformations of thought brought about by social movements.[15] But it is mainly historians who contrast pre- and postmovement cultural ideas. Although they do not use frame language, they make clear that to have any kind of lasting effect, social movements must develop new social values that give new meaning to everyday life, and they must work to get those ideas so widely adopted that most members of the general public "naturally" employ them to evaluate their society.[16]

Of course, no social movements ever build frames entirely from scratch; the principles they use include already-existing cultural concepts. But to become a social movement frame, the various concepts have to be newly articulated, heightened in intensity, combined with previously unrelated ideas, given different emphases, and forged into a coherent whole. This process is easiest to observe in the environmental movement because environmentalism is so new. As we see in Chapter Three, the new frame began to take shape in the 1960s when a group of visionaries appropriated the ecological concept of interconnectedness, put it together with the semireligious tenet that nature should be exalted, and added the political idea that nature is critically endangered. The frame devised from these ideas gives a moral imperative to protecting nature. It allows people to use concepts such as justice in discussing the environment. It repositions questions about things such as forestry, fishing, and waste disposal, claiming them from the scientific realm of true and false and the management realm of effective and ineffective and moving them to the ethical realm of right and wrong.

The literature on social movement framing does not deny that movements create frames. Many scholars in the field recognize that movements introduce new ways of thinking about the world. As Snow and Benford put it in an essay on framing, "[W]e see movement organizations and actors as actively engaged in the production and maintenance of meaning for constituents, antagonists, bystanders or observers."[17] Yet from that recognition, frame theorists move too quickly and directly to the ways movement organizations use frames, skimming over their production and promotion. In making this move, frame theorists neglect what may be a social movement's most important achievement. If a movement actually creates a set of ideas that give new meaning to the world, if it spreads those new ideas so widely that they become familiar to the general public (Snow and Benford's "constituents, antagonists, bystanders or observers"), who then re-understand the events in their lives—if it does those things, the movement has accomplished a great deal more than mobilize people into protest groups. It has initiated social change.

Framing theorists are not the only scholars who slight this major achievement. Other students of social movements do the same thing. For example, Karl-Werner Brand says that social movements flourish "in times of spreading cultural criticism. Such times heighten public sensitivity to the problems of industrialization, urbanization, commercialization, and bureaucratization."[18] Ronald Inglehart states that a major reason for the rise of the ecology movement is that "the public has become more sensitive to the quality of the environment than it was a generation ago."[19] Stephen Cotgrove and Andrew Duff write, "The environmental movement... has provided a vehicle for harnessing beliefs about environmental dangers to support an attack on the central values and beliefs of industrial capitalism."[20]

These scholars all gloss over the agent of change. Brand does not tell us who or what, besides the "times" spreads cultural criticism and heightens public sensitivity to problems. Inglehart ignores the question of why the public is now more sensitive to the quality of the environment. Cotgrove and Duff's language suggests that the beliefs about environmental dangers that are "harnessed" originate outside the movement. In other words, by assuming that the values and meanings that drive social movements predate those movements, these authors close off the possibility that movements themselves could transform people's ways of thinking. Having closed off the possibility, they inevitably fail to ask how movements do transform thinking.

Hegemony

Possibly one reason so many social movement scholars shy away from analyzing movements in this manner is that the analysis raises questions of legitimacy. The social movement literature has been celebrating movements since the 1960s, but should movements be applauded if they in some shrewd way mess around with people's minds? The ability to do so has usually been laid to elites seeking to dominate the masses. Consider Steven Lukes's distinction among three kinds of power. One is the power of A to get B to do something B does not want to do. Another is the power of A to keep B's issues off the political agenda. A third is the power of A to influence, shape, or determine B's very wants and desires. Lukes argues that although the first two kinds of power are weighty in any society, the ability to affect what other people long for is the most consequential sort of power. Such control can prevent people from even thinking thoughts that would challenge the status quo. Is it not, Lukes asks, "the supreme exercise of power to get another or others to have the desires you want them to have—that is, to secure their compliance by controlling their thoughts and desires?"[21]

Lukes, of course, is indebted to Antonio Gramsci's concept of hegemony. Gramsci, influenced in turn by Marx, saw that dominate groups in a society can exercise authority over the general population by convincing them that, however much they may dislike the extant distribution of power and wealth, the distribution is just and immutable. Most people simply assume, he says, that "everything that exists... should exist, that it could not do otherwise than exist." And, although subordinate people do at times desire change and rebel, most people's views of the world mimic the views of the powerful. In Gramsci's words, the mass of society usually adopts "a conception which is not its own but is borrowed from another group; and it affirms this conception verbally and believes itself to be following it, because that is the conception which it follows in 'normal times'—that is, when its conduct is not independent and autonomous, but submissive and subordinate."[22]

More recent scholarship develops Gramsci's theme. Michel Foucault, for example, demonstrated the power of discourse to sustain dominant regimes. He was little interested in the obvious means that states employ to control citizens. To him, the important power is latent in language. He said that "manifold relations of power... permeate, characterize, and constitute the social body, and these relations cannot themselves be established, consolidated, nor implemented without the production, accumulation, circulation and functioning of a discourse."[23] Pierre Bourdieu added to this kind of thinking about power with his concept of "habitus." He showed how the everyday ways societies organize space and time reproduce dominant ideas about the social roles people are expected to fill. "Systems of classification which reproduce, in their own specific logic, the objective classes, i.e., the divisions by sex, age, or position in the relations of production, [reflect a logic in which] the natural and social world appears as self-evident."[24]

As important as these analyses have been to our understanding of quiesence, we should examine the other side of the coin as well. The power to influence what others believe and desire can also be employed, as all these philosophers know, with the intent of redressing injustice. Thus, it is possible to construe hegemonic ideas positively and to inquire into their sources, not in order to free people from disguised oppressors, but to better understand progressive social change. And a few social movement scholars—surprisingly few—have taken on this project.

Reverse Hegemony

One such scholar is Carl Boggs, who argues that social movements "constitute counterhegemonic struggles in the Gramscian sense" when they advance "an alternative ideological framework that subverts the dominant patterns of thought and action."[25] Boggs notes profound, progressive changes that have occurred in Western cultures since the 1960s—widespread new ideas about the relation between the sexes, the legitimacy of authority, the necessity of participation, the value of work, the concept of progress—and attributes the changes in large part to today's social movements.[26]

Boggs's perspective is important precisely because it directs the Gramscian analysis toward social movements, treating them as agents of cultural change rather than as reflections of it. His perspective is important also because it challenges the Marxist idea that political-economic structures are impenetrable without revolution. There are two weaknesses to Boggs's analysis, however. One is its tight focus. It adopts the Gramscian concept of counterhegemony wherein the new consciousness primarily influences and empowers subordinate groups; it thus pays little attention to the consciousness of the general citizenry. A second weakness is its vagueness about how social movements actually influence people's thoughts. From Boggs's account, it is hard to picture just what it is that social movements do.

Thomas Rochon provides more help in understanding how social movements affect culture. Like Boggs, Rochon calls attention to the changed cultural ideas characterizing the end of the twentieth century—changes, he says, "that are individually and collectively so fundamental as to constitute a remaking of American society in the span of a single generation." To account for the changes, Rochon offers a two-step process. The first step is taken by "critical communities." These communities, composed primarily of academics and independent writers, are "networks of people who think intensively about a particular problem and who develop over time a shared understanding of how to view that problem."[27] The shared understanding sharply challenges conventional wisdom and implies the need for major changes in public policies. The second step is taken by people outside the critical communities who pick up the shared understanding and form social movement organizations to disseminate the new ideas to the general public. In Rochon's words:

> The role of social movements in the process of cultural change is to bring the new ideas of critical communities to a wide audience. Movements coalesce around the perspectives developed in the critical communities, and they reformulate those perspectives into terms that will be effective in mobilizing activists and winning social and political allies.... The critical community is interested primarily in the development of new values; the movement is interested in winning social and political acceptance for those values. While the critical community operates mainly through communication within a network of people engaged in conceptual clarification and empirical analysis of a problem, the primary tools of the movement lie in collective action.[28]

Rochon offers three case studies. The first, on desegregation, demonstrates that social movements do indeed affect cultural values. Rochon describes the dramatic changes in public opinion about race that began in the mid–1950s. The seeds for change were sown by a critical community of anthropologists, sociologists, educators, and psychologists whose great volume of research demonstrated that there are no inherent differences among races. The change followed the 1954 Supreme Court decision in *Brown vs. Board of Education,* which drew on those studies. But survey research shows that neither the studies by the critical community nor the court decision directly explains the change in public opinion. Instead, the cultural change is correlated with the mobilizations of the civil rights movement.

Rochon's second case study, on sexual harassment, somewhat muddies his two-step model, putting the work of critical communities in the context of ongoing social movements. He traces the concept of sexual harassment to a group of feminist lawyers and scholars in the 1970s and 1980s and shows that they not only created the concept but worked to get it widely diffused throughout society. Their strategy was to file complaints within the Equal Employment Opportunity Commission and the criminal justice system. The strategy worked in that media coverage of the complaints helped to make the public familiar with the concept. At the same time, feminists not linked directly to the critical community spread the concept of sexual harassment through public meetings and demonstrations. The concept, of course, got a huge boost when Anita Hill testified at the Senate hearings on Clarence Thomas's Supreme Court nomination. But Rochon argues that none of this would have happened, or at least it would not have had the same impact, had not the feminist movement already been working for years to promote the idea of gender equality.

Rochon's third case study, on alcohol abuse, shows that when different critical communities redefine social problems, different kinds of social movements follow. Alcohol abuse has attracted the attention of a succession of critical communities, who have seen it as an addiction (a view that prompted the formation of the temperance movement), as a disease (a view that gave rise to Alcoholics Anonymous), and as a problem only when it affects other people (a view that inspired Mothers Against Drunk Driving).

Rochon goes on to examine the factors that draw people to social movement organizations and the factors that make the organizations successful. In doing so, he offers more descriptions of the ways movement organizations promote the ideas of critical communities. The descriptions are not particularly surprising (he emphasizes the use of the media and the formation of ties with political leaders), and Rochon does not expect them to be. His principal contribution to social movement studies is his argument, carefully documented and beautifully written, that movements produce culture change, and his description of how that change occurs.

My own study of the environmental movement, however, suggests that Rochon's division between critical communities and social movements is too sharp. As I note, Rochon himself seems to question the division in his story about sexual harassment. In his final chapter, however, he underscores the distinction once more. Such a division between thinkers and doers makes scientists such as Rachel Carson and Barry Commoner not part of the environmental movement but only stimulators of it. By the same token, it leaves no clear place for people like William Cronon and Daniel Botkin, self-described promoters of environmentalism who are also part of an ongoing critical community. Rochon does say that some people are both social critics and movement activists. But his example is Martin Luther King, Jr., and the activism of Cronon and Botkin is hardly analogous to King's. My study also suggests that Rochon defines social movements too narrowly. He thinks of movements as organizations that form to mobilize supporters and to spread the new ideas of critical communities. The definition fits nicely with mainstream environmental groups such as the Natural Resources Defense Council. It has less pertinence for the people I am most concerned with in this book and to whom I return in the last two sections of this chapter: nonorganizational actors such as scientists: and members of grassroots organizations who do not align themselves with the environmental movement. These people have played substantial roles in the task of creating and spreading environmental ideas. Unless they and similar actors are included in the concept of social movement, it is hard to explain environmentalism's impact on culture.

For an approach to social movements closer to the one I am edging up on here, an approach with a broader definition of social movement actor, it is helpful to examine the work of Ron Eyerman and Andrew Jamison. Like Rochon, they see social movements as influencers of consciousness, and like him they see a community of intellectuals as playing a significant role in initiating movements. But they argue that, as movements develop, the distinction between thinkers and doers blurs. The argument follows from their concept "of social movements as forms of cognitive praxis which are shaped by both external and internal political processes."[29]

Movements, say Eyerman and Jamison, are not things so much as public spaces in which human knowledge is produced. "It is precisely in the creation, articulation, formulation of new thoughts and ideas—new knowledge—that a social movement defines itself in society." Whereas some of this new knowledge is easily traceable to the intellectuals who first articulate movement ideas, much of the knowledge comes from what Eyerman and Jamison call "movement intellectuals." These are professionals of one sort of another whose ways of construing the world and whose ways of behaving professionally have been deeply influenced by movement ideas and values. Bringing movement ideas into their professional lives, movement intellectuals affect not only their own professions but also the thinking of large numbers of other people as well. In Eyerman and Jamison's words, their "very professional skills are formed by the needs and interests... of social movements. It is in this way, by carving out spaces for new intellectual 'types' or roles to develop that social movements help reform intellectual life itself."[30]

Eyerman and Jamison describe several different kinds of movement intellectuals. Some are "counterexperts" who challenge the decisions and standards of government experts. In the environmental movement, the counterexperts are biologists and biology students, lawyers and law students, physicians and medical students. These movement intellectuals have not only produced new research findings but also have disputed "the elitist conception of knowledge epitomized by state experts." Other movement intellectuals are "grassroots engineers," who direct "a kind of sociotechnical learning process." Environmentalist grassroots engineers teach "short courses in renewable energy, alternative agriculture, recycling, etc." In the process of doing so they also "articulate... the identity of the environmental movement." Still other movement intellectuals are "public educators" who popularize the movement. Some "specialize in public speaking, others in writing, still others in media, debating with the opposition, the established energy officials and environmental authorities."[31] The goal of all these movement intellectuals is to recruit people not to organizations but to ideas—the new ideas about how we should live and how we should relate to one another that lie at the heart of social movements.

Although Eyerman and Jamison's book suffers at times from vagueness and its high level of abstraction results in some conflicting definitions of terms, its construal of social movements as cognitive praxis makes room within movements for the full panoply of actors. If social movements are producers of ideas, then everyone who adds to that production is part of the movement.

Social Movement Actors

From a similar view of social movements, I have been arguing that, for the environmental movement, certain scientists constitute one group of movement actors. There are men and women who see exposure to industrial wastes within an environmentalist frame. Embracing ideas initially developed by Rachel Carson and others about the probable effects of synthetic compounds on the human body, they assume that exposure is likely to be hazardous and they employ their scientific expertise to investigate that likelihood. In doing so, they take somewhat different approaches from investigators who, uninfluenced by environmentalism, assume that exposure is likely to be safe. I give some examples in Chapter Four: Environmentalist scientists have developed the idea that some industrial pollutants are endocrine disrupters; they have used the experiences of children instead of adults, and minorities instead of whites, to measure the impact of toxins on human health; they have looked beyond exposures to single chemicals and have taken a "chemical soup" as their object of study; they have expanded the concept of disease; they have questioned the standard of proof. These different approaches make the discovery of correlations between exposure to pollution and disease more likely. When such correlations are found, the research makes the environmentalist view of the world more incontrovertible.

The environmentalist scientists who do this research are thus actors in the environmental movement. But they do not quite fit into Rochon's scheme or into Eyerman and Jamison's. They are neither the critical community who started the movement nor the members of movement organizations trying to mobilize supporters. They neither dispute the state's concept of knowledge, nor teach courses and give speeches. (Or, if they do any of those things, they are double-actors.) The scientists are actors because in their work they fortify the principles fostered by the environmental movement. Each one of their studies showing a correlation between disease and exposure to industrial toxins provides new reason to see nature as interconnected, to believe that human interference in nature can be harmful, and to conclude that modern society is in a state of crisis. The work of these scientists, influenced in the first place by environmentalism, thus strengthens the environmentalist frame. It makes the principles constituting the frame more commonsensical. As a result, the frame becomes more serviceable. Environmentalists can use it to explain more conditions or events, and the general public is more likely to find the frame a logical way to order their experiences.

Seeing social movements as creators and promoters of ideas instead of as only collections of organizations brings into focus many more movement actors besides scientists. It is commonplace now to recognize the importance of the media in social movements.[32] And, although some journalists report favorably on movement activities because they think the reports will attract readers or listeners, others are adherents of social movements and use their professional position to promote them. Two of my studies offer clear examples. The *New Yorker* writer Paul Brodeur used the situation in Guilford to write more about his long-time passionate concern about the dangers of exposure to electromagnetic fields. At Love Canal, a journalist for the *Niagara Gazette,* Michael Brown, had begun warning readers about the leaking waste dump long before the Love Canal Homeowners Association was formed, and he remained an association ally throughout the entire two-year protest. He subsequently wrote a book that put Love Canal in the context of a whole range of environmental disasters.[33] Both journalists helped expand environmental issues to include exposure to industrial toxins. Their work thus reinforced movement principles and made them relevant to new groups of citizens.

There also are governmental actors. Some legislators and bureaucrats are hostile to social movements or search out neutral positions or feign love of nature to get votes, but others are dedicated proponents. In fact, the scholarly literature on political opportunity recognizes this phenomenon and describes the important role that elected and appointed officials can play in advancing movement goals. A good example is Senator Gaylord Nelson, who conceived of Earth Day 1970 and worked to make it happen, thus broadcasting environmentalist principles to an enormous audience. That a senator would play such a prominent part should be surprising only to people who believe that social movements consist of clubs.

Other professionals, too, become social movement actors. Lawyers, as Thomas Rochon shows,[34] broadened and strengthened the feminist movement when they developed the concept of sexual harrassment. And, as I noted in Chapter Three, environmental movement actors can be found in commerce, in schools, and in religious organizations. They run ecotourism businesses. They open stores to sell products linked to the protection of nature. They teach or preach environmentalism. Again, some of these people may be cynics. Businesspeople may be out to make a buck on what they assume is a passing fad. Educators and religious leaders may not themselves be very moved by nature's plight; they just like to link their lessons to current topics. But environmentalist sentiment is now far too widespread in this country to allow for a generalization of such opportunism to all businesspeople, educators, and clergy. And ironically enough, even opportunists become movement actors. They take advantage of environmentalism's popularity for self-gain, but in doing so they also promote the movement. Without really meaning to, they aid environmentalists in the great task of transforming the movement's once-alien ideas into plain common sense. Similar to sincere environmentalists, the opportunists help turn environmentalism into an "intuitive" way for people to understand the world around them.

To the above list we could add other movement actors who are not necessarily associated with environmental organizations. The actors include Congressional staffers who talk up environmentalism to the senators and congresspeople they work for, architects who encourage their clients to desire "environmentally friendly" buildings, and farmers who discuss organic farming with other cultivators.

We could also add all the men and women who do such things as put recycling bins out on their curbs for pickup, defend environmentalist principles in conversations with friends and family or wear t-shirts with environmentalist slogans. These are tiny acts, and from one perspective they are simply indicators that the general public embraces environmentalism. But from another perspective, these are acts that promote the movement. The recycling bins are symbols of environmental problems and solutions. The conversations are lessons. The t-shirts are walking billboards. Each act in its small way helps to create a culture in which environmentalist principles are taken for granted.

Change

This list of environmental movement players who take action independent of formal movement organizations suggests a view of social movements that is somewhat different from the views of Rochon and Eyerman and Jamison. From all three perspectives one can imagine a stage and an audience. The stage is outdoors in a huge city park where the audience has brought picnics, frisbees, blankets, and folding chairs. In this setting, Rochon describes something like this: on the stage, a few speakers appear and talk to the audience, presenting new ideas about how society is organized and how it should be organized. When the speakers finish, some men and women in the audience, inspired by the new ideas, move from their picnic spots and climb on the stage. There they form into a variety of groups (often with many difficulties, as Rochon shows) and then they restate the speakers' message in more popular forms, using a variety of different stategies and methods. Their goal is to get the rest of the audience, still on their blankets, to attend rallies, pledge money, sign petitions, vote for certain political candidates, support new laws and regulations, and conduct their personal lives in ways reflective of the new ideas.

Eyerman and Jamison describe a similar scenario, but they see the stage occupied not only by the folks who organized into groups but also by unaffiliated professionals, such as engineers, biologists, and educators. For these professionals, the social movement stage is a new public space in which to work. Some are inspired by movement ideas to do new kinds of research and to point out the ideological foundations of the old research. Others use the new space and their professional skills to teach people how to apply movement ideas to their own jobs and personal lives. Still others, drawing on their experience as educators of one sort or another, expound on the ideas the initial speakers presented. The goal of all these professionals is not so much to get the audience to take political action as it is to get them to replace their old ideas about society with new ones.

My own view of the events in the park is similar to that of Eyerman and Jamison, but it encompasses the audience as much as it does the figures on the stage. I see the events on the stage spilling over into the audience. Proponents of the new ideas—members of the organization as well as the unaffiliated professionals—wander around among the people on the grass, chatting with them and sharing their potato salad. At the same time, some members of the audience begin talking to one another about the new ideas. It becomes hard to distinguish the audience from the actors. The straight line of communication in Rochon's scenario, where an initial set of ideas is picked up by organizations and transmitted from there to the general public, gets turned back on itself as people in the general public begin broadcasting the ideas themselves.

Not everyone takes part in this broadcasting of environmental ideas, and certainly not everyone takes part initially. The future members of the grassroots groups I've been writing about frequently pay little conscious attention to the events on the stage. They do not talk about the new ideas with the environmentalists who wander among them, nor do they talk about the ideas with their neighbors. Maybe they are more interested in their friends and family, their picnic, the nearby ball game.

Since the ideas are repeated over and over in dozens of different and creative ways by many different kinds of people, however, they absorb them. Thus, the future grassroots activists are unwitting receivers of environmentalism; it is all around them. When they later discover a polluting industry in their neighborhood, they draw on the assimilated environmentalist principles to understand what it signifies. Or, to use the concepts from earlier in this chapter, the principles become the frame that gives their situation meaning. At the point when they begin to protest against pollution, they, too, become movement actors, for they broadcast the environmentalist idea that human interference in nature is likely to have bad consequences.

This production-in-the-park analogy can not be taken too far. Like most analogies, it gets unwieldy. It also misleads. Social movements are not big shows. In the end, movements are simply what they are. What they are, of course, can never be entirely apparent. Social movements are too large and they lend themselves to too many points of view for that. Observers have to concentrate on only a few aspects at a time. The aspect of social movements that I have emphasized in this book is their ability to change what we take for granted, their ability to make us see the world differently, and thus their ability to kindle social change. To understand how they can have this kind of power we have to recognize all the social movement actors: the visionaries who first articulate movement ideas, the members of organizations who mobilize people around the ideas, and especially, since they are usually forgotten in social movement studies, the untold numbers of men and women outside of movement organizations who foster the ideas on the job, in the street, and at home.

Notes

Overview

1. For a distinction between conservationism and environmentalism see Samuel P. Hays, *Beauty, Health, and Permanence: Environmental Politics in the United States, 1955–1985* (New York: Cambridge University Press, 1987).

2. Benjamin A. Goldman, *The Truth about Where You Live* (New York: Times Books, 1991), 169.

3. Council on Environmental Quality, Executive Office of the President, *Environmental Quality: 1994–1995 Report* (Washington, D.C., n.d.), 371. The CEQ report continues, "Air emissions accounted for 69 percent of the total; followed by underground injection (much of it controlled release into subsurface wells) at 15 percent, releases to landfills and other types of land disposal at 13 percent, and releases to water at 3 percent."

4. Ibid., p. 87.

5. Goldman, *The Truth about Where You Live*, pp. 186–87.

6. Council on Environmental Quality, *Environmental Quality*, p. 96.

7. See figure 5.2, p. 83, in ibid. Water from the approximately 10.5 million private wells in the United States is not included in this figure. See also Anne Nadakavukaren, *Our Global Environment: A Health Perspective*, 4th ed. (Prospect Heights, Ill.: Waveland Press, 1995), 555.

8. Council on Environmental Quality, *Environmental Quality*, p. 365.

9. Ibid., figure 6.1, p. 111.

10. Commission for Racial Justice, *Toxic Waste and Race in the United States* (New York: United Church of Christ, 1987), xiv.

Chapter One: Protest against Pollution

1. From Robert Gottlieb's perspective, mobilization against environmental pollution began at the turn of the twentieth century, inspired by Jane Addams and other urban reformers. (See Robert Gottlieb, *Forcing the Spring: The Transformation of the American Environmental Movement* [Washington, D.C.: Island Press, 1993]). However, I see no evidence that the current activism against environmental pollution is an extension or a reanimation of that earlier struggle. Instead, as I argue in Chapter Three, it springs from a new framework for understanding nature, developed in the middle of the century.

2. Sidney Verba, *Participation and Political Equality: A Seven-Nation Comparison* (New York: Cambridge University Press, 1978); Doug McAdam, "The Framing Function of Movement Tactics: Strategic Dramaturgy in the American Civil Rights Movement," in *Comparative Perspectives on Social Movements: Political Opportunities, Mobilizing Structures, and Cultural Framings,* ed. Doug McAdam, John D. McCarthy, and Mayer N. Zald (New York: Cambridge University Press, 1996).

3. Carol Pateman, *Participation and Democracy* (Cambridge: Cambridge University Press, 1970); Jack DeSario and Stuart Langton, eds., *Citizen Participation in Public Decision Making* (New York: Greenwood Press, 1987).

4. Alberto Melucci, *Nomads of the Present: Social Movements and Individual Needs in Contemporary Society* (Philadelphia: Temple University Press, 1989); Verta Taylor and Nancy E. Whittier, "Collective Identity in Social Movement Communities: Lesbian Feminist Mobilization," in *Frontiers in Social Movement Theory,* ed. John D. Morris and Carol McClurg Mueller (New Haven, Conn.: Yale University Press, 1992).

5. Jeffrey M. Berry, *The Interest Group Society* (New York: HarperCollins, 1989); Harry C. Boyte, Heather Booth, and Steve Max, *Citizen Action and the New American Populism* (Philadelphia: Temple University Press, 1986); Benjamin Barber, *Strong Democracy: Participatory Politics for a New Age* (Berkeley: University of California Press, 1984).

6. Interview with Bob Hemstock in Guilford, Connecticut, December 3, 1990.

7. Telephone interview with Carolyn Jean Dupuy, June 6, 1996.

8. Paul Brodeur, "Calamity on Meadow Street," *New Yorker,* 9 July 1990, 38–71.

9. Paul Brodeur, *Currents of Death* (New York: Simon and Schuster, 1989).

10. Richard Stone, "Polarized Debate: EMFs and Cancer," *Science* 258 (1992): 1724–25.

11. In a letter to David R. Brown, chief epidemiologist at the Connecticut Department of Health Services (CDHS), *New Yorker* editor Robert Gottlieb wrote, "We have received many calls and letters asking for more information about the possible EMF health hazards." The letter is dated November 6, 1990 and is in the files of CDHS.

12. Nancy Wertheimer and Ed Leeper, "Electrical Wiring Configurations and Childhood Cancer," *American Journal of Epidemiology* 109 (1979): 273–84.

13. Nancy Wertheimer and Ed Leeper, "Adult Cancer Related to Electrical Wires Near the Home," *International Journal of Epidemiology* 11 (1982): 345–55.

14. John P. Fulton, Sidney Cobb, Lorenna Preble, Louis Leone, and Edwin Forman, "Electrical Wiring Configurations and Childhood Leukemia in Rhode Island," *American Journal of Epidemiology* 111 (1980): 292–96. See also Nancy Wertheimer, "Re: Electrical Wiring Configurations and Childhood Leukemia in Rhode Island," [Letter] *American Journal of Epidemiology* 111 (1980): 461–62.

15. Lennart Tomenius, "50-Hz Electromagnetic Environment and the Incidence of Childhood Tumors in Stockholm County," *Bioelectromagnetics* 7 (1986): 191–207.

16. Indira Nair, "Biological Effects of Power Frequency Electric and Magnetic Fields," background paper for U.S. Congress, Office of Technology Assessment, 1989; Michael Coleman and Valerie Beral, "A Review of the Epidemiological Studies of the Health Effects of Living Near or Working with Electricity Generation and Transmission Equipment," *International Journal of Epidemiology* 17 (1988): 1–13. The number of articles I have been able to locate (nine) showing a relation between health and exposure to EMFs is small compared with the 130 that Hemstock found. I imagine that Hemstock did not distinguish among peer-reviewed studies, surveys of the literature, and articles in the popular literature.

17. Interview in Guilford, December 13, 1990.

18. Roger M. Macklis, "Magnetic Healing, Quackery, and the Debate about the Health Effects of Electromagnetic Fields," *Annals of Internal Medicine* 118 (1993): 376–83; James C. Lin, "Perspectives on Health Effects of Electric and Magnetic Fields," *Perceptual and Motor Skills* 72 (1991): 249–50.

19. T. S. Tenforde, "Biological Interactions and Potential Health Effects of Extremely Low-Frequency Magnetic Fields from Power Lines and Other Common Sources," *Annual Review of Public Health* 13 (1992): 173–96.

20. M. Granger Morgan, "Alternative Functional Relationships between EMF Field Exposure and Possible Health Effects: Report on an Expert Workshop," *Bioelectromagnetics* 13 (1992): 335–50.

21. Jack Siemiatycki, "Problems and Priorities in Epidemiological Research on Human Health: Effects Related to Wiring Code and Electric and Magnetic Fields," *Environmental Health Perspectives* 101, Suppl. 4 (1993): 135–41.

22. Bengt Knave, "Electric and Magnetic Fields and Health Outcomes—An Overview," *Scandinavian Journal of Work and Environmental Health* 20 Spec. (1994): 78–89.

23. Martha S. Linet, Elizabeth E. Hatch, Ruth A. Kleinerman, Leslie L. Robison, William T. Kaune, Dana R. Friedman, Richard K. Severson, Carol M. Haines, Charleen R. Hartsock, Shelly Niwa, Sholom Wacholder, and Robert T. Tarone, "Residential Exposure to Magnetic Fields and Acute Lymphoblastic Leukemia in Children," *New England Journal of Medicine* 337 (1997): 1–7.

24. National Research Council, *Possible Health Effects of Exposure to Residential Electric and Magnetic Fields* (Washington, D.C.: National Academy Press, 1997).

25. Quoted in Stone, "Polarized Debate."

26. These are unpublished findings. The department stated them in a "fact sheet" distributed at the meeting and in a letter to the editor that appeared in the Manchester, Connecticut, *Journal Inquirer* on September 8, 1990. They can also be found in Paul Brodeur, "Department of Amplification," *New Yorker,* 8 November 1990.

27. Telephone conversation with Bob Hemstock, November 21, 1990.

28. Telephone conversation with Bob Hemstock, June 9, 1992.

29. Unless indicated otherwise, the information on the Alsea case is from Carol Van Strum, *A Bitter Fog* (San Francisco: Sierra Club, 1983).

30. Interview with Carol Van Strum in Tidewater, Oregon, September 3, 1996.

31. Ibid.

32. Van Strum, *A Bitter Fog*, p. 95.

33. Interview with Carol Van Strum in Tidewater, Oregon, September 3, 1996.

34. Quoted in Van Strum, *A Bitter Fog*, p. 164.

35. Quoted in ibid., pp. 164–65.

36. Quoted in ibid., p. 165.

37. Robert D. McFadden, "EPA, Citing Miscarriages, Restricts Two Herbicides," *New York Times,* 2 March 1979; p. A10; Jeffrey Smith, "EPA Halts Most Use of Herbicide 2,4,5,-T," *Science* 203 (1979):1090–91.

38. Environmental Protection Agency, "Health Assessment Document for 2,3,7,8-Tetrachlorodinbenzo-p-Dioxin (TCDD) and Related Compounds," draft, 1994. As of February 2000, the report had not yet been issued in final form.

39. See Van Strum, *A Bitter Fog*, pp. 168–69.

40. Environmental Protection Agency, "Health Assessment Document for 2,3,7,8-Tetrachlorodinbenzo-p-Dioxin (TCDD) and Related Compounds," p. 258.

41. Telephone interview, April 22, 1997. The toxicologist asked me not to identify him.

42. Lois Marie Gibbs, "What to Expect from Industry," in *Dying from Dioxin: A Citizen's Guide to Reclaiming Our Health and Rebuilding Democracy* (Boston: South End Press, 1995), 124.

43. Samuel Epstein, *Hazardous Waste in America* (San Francisco: Sierra Club Books, 1982); Lois Marie Gibbs, *Love Canal: My Story* (Albany: State University of New York Press, 1982); Adeline Gordon Levine, *Love Canal: Science, Politics, and People* (Lexington, Mass.: Lexington Books, 1982); Martha R. Fowlkes and Patricia Y. Miiler, "Chemicals and

Community at Love Canal," in *The Social and Cultural Construction of Risk*, ed. Brandon B. Johnson and Vincent T. Covello (Dordrecht, The Netherlands: D. Reidel, 1987); Gerald B. Silverman, "Love Canal: A Retrospective," *Environmental Reporter*, Bureau of National Affairs 20, no. 20 (1989): pt. 2; Allan Mazur, *A Hazardous Inquiry: The Rashomon Effect at Love Canal* (Cambridge, Mass.: Harvard University Press, 1998).

44. New York Department of Health, "Love Canal: Public Health Time Bomb," Special report to the governor and legislature, 1978, pp. 6, 11, 12, 14.

45. Gibbs, *Love Canal*, p. 15.

46. Ibid., p. 30.

47. Levine, *Love Canal;* Silverman, "Love Canal"; Andrew Szasz, *EcoPopulism: Toxic Waste and the Movement for Environmental Justice* (Minneapolis: University of Minnesota Press, 1994).

48. Clark W. Heath, "Field Epidemiologic Studies of Populations Exposed to Waste Dumps," *Environmental Health Perspectives* 48 (1983): 6.

49. National Research Council, *Environmental Epidemiology: Public Health and Hazardous Waste*, vol. 1 (Washington, D.C.: National Academy Press, 1991).

50. Dwight T. Janerich, William S. Burnett, Gerald Feck, Margaret Hoff, Phillip Nasca, Anthony P. Polednak, Peter Greenwald, and Nicholas Vianna, "Cancer Incidence in the Love Canal Area," *Science* 212 (1981): 1404–7.

51. Nicholas J. Vianna and Adele K. Polan, "Incidence of Low Birth Weight among Love Canal Residents," *Science* 226 (1984): 1217–19.

52. Lynn R. Goldman, Beverly Paigen, Mary M. Magnant, and Joseph H. Highland, "Low Birth Weight, Prematurity, and Birth Defects in Children Living Near the Hazardous Waste Site, Love Canal," *Hazardous Waste and Hazardous Materials* 2 (1985): 209–223.

53. Beverly Paigen, Lynn R. Goldman, Joseph H. Highland, Mary M. Magnant, and A. T. Steegman Jr., "Prevalence of Health Problems in Children Living Near Love Canal," *Hazardous Waste and Hazardous Materials* 2 (1985): 23–43.

54. Dante Picciano, "Pilot Cytogenic Study of the Residents Living Near Love Canal: A Hazardous Waste Site," *Mammalian Chromosome Newsletter* 21 (1980): 86–93.

55. See Gina Kolata, "Love Canal: False Alarm Caused by Botched Study," *Science* 208 (1980): 1239–42.

56. Clark W. Heath Jr., Marion R. Nadel, Matthew M. Zack Jr., Andrew T. L. Chen, Michael A. Bender, and R. Julian Preston, "Cytogenic Findings in Persons Living Near Love Canal," *Journal of the American Medical Association* 251 (1984): 1437–40.

57. I was given their names from a spokesperson at the Center for Health, Environment and Justice in Falls Church, Virginia. The conversations lasted twenty minutes to an hour. For more on these women's recollections, see Sylvia N. Tesh, "Framing Love Canal: The Environmental Movement Trumps the Public Health Movement" (paper presented at the annual meeting of the American Political Science Association, Washington, D.C., August 1997).

58. The 8,000 figure comes from the organization's quarterly publication, *Everyone's Backyard* 15, no. 1 (spring 1997).

59. Sheldon Krimsky and Alonzo Plough, *Environmental Hazards: Communicating Risks As a Social Process* (Dover, Mass.: Auburn House, 1988).

60. Michael Gough, *Dioxin, Agent Orange: The Facts* (New York: Plenum Press, 1986).

61. Phil Brown and Edwin J. Mikkelsen, *No Safe Place: Toxic Waste, Leukemia, and Community Action* (Berkeley: University of California Press, 1990); Jonathan Harr, *A Civil Action* (New York: Vintage Books, 1996); Paula DiPerna, *Cluster Mystery: Epidemic and the Children of Woburn, Mass.* (St. Louis: C.B. Mosby, 1985).

62. Kai Erickson, *A New Species of Trouble: Explorations in Disaster, Trauma, and Community* (New York: W.W. Norton, 1994).

63. See Raymond L. Goldsteen and John K. Schorr, *Demanding Democracy after Three Mile Island* (Gainesville: University of Florida Press, 1991). The Three Mile Island case has been the subject of fresh controversy. A 1990 study finding no excess cancer at Three Mile Island, was challenged in 1997 by Steve Wing and colleagues, who reanalyzed the data used in the earlier study and concluded that radiation doses at TMI are related to increased cancer incidence. See Steve Wing, David Richardson, Donna Armstrong, and Douglas Crawford-Brown, "A Re-evaluation of Cancer Incidence Near the Three Mile Island Nuclear Plant: The Collision of Evidence and Assumptions," *Environmental Health Perspectives* 105 (1997): 52–57. For a discussion, see the "Correspondence" section of *Environmental Health Perspectives* 105, nos. 1, 3, 6 (1997). See also Seth Tuler, "Review of 'A Reevaluation of Cancer Incidence Near the Three Mile Island Nuclear Plant: The Collision of Evidence and Assumptions,'" *CCRI: The Childhood Cancer Research Institute* (August 1997): 1–5.

64. National Research Council, *Environmental Epidemiology*.

65. See Gibbs. "What to Expect from Industry." Another place to find this theme is in *RACHEL's Environment and Health Weekly*, a newsletter by Peter Montague. It is available by mail from the Environmental Research Foundation, P. O. Box 5036, Annapolis, MD 21403, and by e-mail (peter@rachel.clark.net). My strong impression from talking with grassroots activists is that the newsletter is widely read. Montague refuses to divulge the newsletter's circulation.

66. Goldsteen and Schorr, *Demanding Democracy after Three Mile Island;* Michael R. Edelstein, *Contaminated Communities: The Social and Psychological Impacts of Residential Toxic Exposure* (Boulder, Colo.: Westview Press, 1988); Szasz, *EcoPopulism*.

67. Paul Slovic, "Perception of Risk," *Science* 236 (1987): 280–85; Paul Slovic, Baruch Fischhoff, and Sarah Lichtenstein, "Perceived Risk: Psychological Factors and Social Implications," *Proceedings of the Royal Society of London. Series A* (1981): 376. I discuss this literature in Chapter Five.

68. Edith Efron, *Apocalyptics: Cancer and the Big Lie: How Environmental Politics Controls What We Know about Cancer* (New York: Simon and Schuster, 1984); Michael Fumento, *Science under Siege: Balancing Technology and the Environment* (New York: William Morrow, 1993); Elizabeth M. Whelan, *Toxic Terror: The Truth behind the Cancer Scares* (Buffalo, N.Y.: Prometheus Books, 1993); Aaron Wildavsky, *But Is It True? A Citizen's Guide to Environmental Health and Safety Issues* (Cambridge, Mass.: Harvard University Press, 1995).

Chapter Two: Environmental Health Research

1. National Research Council, *Science and Judgement in Risk Assessment* (Washington, D.C.: Taylor and Francis, 1996).

2. William D. Ruckelshaus, "Risk, Science, and Democracy," *Issues in Science and Technology*, 2 (1985): 19–38; Jacqueline Patterson, Steven Lutkenhoff, and William Rush, "Use of Health Risk Estimates in U.S. EPA Activities," in *The Analysis, Communication, and Perception of Risk*, ed. B. John Garrick and William C. Gekler (New York: Plenum Press, 1991); U.S. Congress, Office of Technology Assessment, *Researching Health Risks* (Washington, D.C., 1993).

3. Ruckelshaus, "Risk, Science, and Democracy," p. 28.

4. *National Environmental Policy Act of 1969, U.S. Code*, vol. 42, sec. 4321 (1970).

5. Barry Commoner, "Pollution Prevention: Putting Comparative Risk Assessment in Its Place," in *Worst Things First? The Debate over Risk-Based National Environmental Priorities*, ed. Adam M. Finkel and Dominic Golding (Washington, D.C.: Resources for the Future, 1994); Sandra Steingraber, "Mechanisms, Proof, and Unmet Needs: The Perspective of a Cancer Activist," *Environmental Health Perspectives* 105, Suppl. 3 (1997): 685–87; Al Alm, "Why We Didn't Use 'Risk' Before," *EPA Journal* 17, no. 2 (1991): 13–16.

6. National Research Council, *Science and Judgement in Risk Assessment*, p. 26.

7. Nicholas Ashford, "An Innovation-Based Strategy for the Environment," in Finkel and Golding, *Worst Things First?*

8. National Research Council, *Risk Assessment in the Federal Government: Managing the Process* (Washington, D.C.: National Academy Press, 1983).

9. Robert Ginsburg, "Quantitative Risk Assessment and the Illusion of Safety," *New Solutions* 3, no. 2 (1993): 8–15.

10. Samuel S. Epstein, *The Politics of Cancer* (San Francisco: Sierra Club Books, 1978); Robert N. Proctor, *Cancer Wars: How Politics Shapes What We Know and Don't Know about Cancer* (New York: Basic Books, 1995).

11. Raymond W. Tennant, Michael D. Shelby, Errol Zeiger, Joseph K. Haseman, Judson Spalding, William Caspary, Michael Resnick, Stanley Stasiewicz, Beth Anderson, and Robert Minor, "Prediction of Chemical Carcinogenicity in Rodents from In Vitro Genetic Toxicity Assays," *Science* 236 (1987): 933–41.

12. U.S. Congress, Office of Technology Assessment, *Identifying and Regulating Carcinogens* (Washington, D.C., 1987).

13. National Research Council, *Science and Judgement in Risk Assessment*, p. 94.

14. Epstein, *The Politics of Cancer*, p. 66; Proctor, *Cancer Wars*, p. 167.

15. National Research Council, *Science and Judgement in Risk Assessment*, p. 92.

16. Environmental Protection Agency, "Health Assessment Document for 2,3,7,8-Tetrachlorodibenzo-p-Dioxin (TCDD) and Related Compounds," draft, (1994), chapter 6.

17. Ibid., chapter 7.

18. Epstein, *The Politics of Cancer*, p. 66.

19. National Research Council, *Science and Judgement in Risk Assessment*, p. 133.

20. U.S. Congress, Office of Technology Assessment, *Identifying and Regulating Carcinogens*, p. 58.

21. Proctor, *Cancer Wars*, 7, Figure 2.

22. National Research Council, *Science and Judgement in Risk Assessment*, chapter 4.

23. Michael Fumento, *Science under Siege: Balancing Technology and the Environment* (New York: William Morrow, 1993); Edith Efron, *Apocalyptics: Cancer and the Big Lie: How Environmental Politics Controls What We Know about Cancer* (New York: Simon and Schuster, 1984); Elizabeth M. Whelan, *Toxic Terror: The Truth behind the Cancer Scares* (Buffalo, N.Y.: Prometheus Books, 1993); Aaron Wildavsky, *But Is it True? A Citizen's Guide to Environmental Health and Safety Issues* (Cambridge, Mass.: Harvard University Press, 1995).

24. Irva Hertz-Picciotto, "Epidemiology and Quantitative Risk Assessment: A Bridge from Science to Policy," *American Journal of Public Health* 85, no. 4 (1995): 484–91.

25. Daniel Wartenberg and Ronald Simon, "Comment: Integrating Epidemiologic Data into Risk Assessment," *American Journal of Public Health* 85, no. 4 (1995): 491–93.

26. Sioban D. Harlow and Martha S. Linet, "Agreement between Questionnaire Data and Medical Records: The Evidence for Accuracy of Recall," *American Journal of Epidemiology* 129 (1989): 233–48.

27. National Research Council, *Environmental Epidemiology: Public Health and Hazardous Waste*, vol. 1 (Washington, D.C.: National Academy Press, 1991).

28. Beverly Paigen, Lynn R. Goldman, Joseph H. Highland, Mary M. Magnant, and A. T. Steegman Jr., "Prevalence of Health Problems in Children Living Near Love Canal," *Hazardous Waste and Hazardous Materials* 2 (1985): 25.

29. Neil A. Holtzman and Muin J. Khoury, "Monitoring for Congenital Malformations," *Annual Review of Public Health* 7 (1986): 127–266.

30. Dwight T. Janerich, William S. Burnett, Gerald Feck, Margaret Hoff, Phillip Nasca, Anthony P. Polednak, Peter Greenwald, and Nicholas Vianna, "Cancer Incidence in the Love Canal," *Science* 212 (1981): 1407.

31. Whelan, *Toxic Terror,* pp. 124–37. [Emphasis in original.]

32. National Research Council, *Environmental Epidemiology;* Gary M. Marsh and Richard J. Caplan, "Evaluating Health Effects of Exposure at Hazardous Waste Sites: A Review of the State-of-the-Art, with Recommendations for Future Research," in *Health Effects from Hazardous Waste Sites,* ed. Julian B. Alderman and Dwight W. Underhill (Chelsea, Mich.: Lewis Publishers, 1987).

33. On dioxin see Michael Gough, *Dioxin, Agent Orange: The Facts* (New York: Plenum Press, 1986). On asbestos see Wildavsky, *But Is it True?*

34. Kenneth Rothman, "A Sobering Start for the Cluster Buster's Conference," *American Journal of Epidemiology* 132 Suppl. 1 (1990): S6–S13.

35. U.S. Congress, Office of Technology Assessment, *Identifying and Regulating Carcinogens.*

36. Raymond Richard Neutra, "Counterpoint from a Cluster Buster," *American Journal of Epidemiology* 132 (1990): 1–8.

37. Dwight T. Janerich et al., "Cancer Incidence in the Love Canal Area," 1407.

38. Rothman, "A Sobering Start for the Cluster Buster's Conference"; Neutra, "Counterpoint from a Cluster Buster."

39. David R. Brown, letter to the Manchester, Connecticut, *Journal Inquirer,* August 31, 1990; David R. Brown, letter to Samuel Milham, September 25, 1990. Both letters are in the files of the Connecticut Department of Health Services.

40. Quoted in Gough, *Dioxin, Agent Orange,* p. 144.

41. National Research Council, *Environmental Epidemiology,* p. 9.

42. For a broader discussion see Philip Landrigan, "Epidemiologic Approaches to Persons with Exposure to Waste Chemicals," *Environmental Health Perspectives* 48 (1983):93–97; Marsh and Caplan, "Evaluating Health Effects of Exposure at Hazardous Waste Sites"; Ken Sexton, Sherry G. Selvan, Diane K. Wagner, and Jeffrey A. Lybarger, "Estimating Human Exposure to Environmental Pollutants: Availability and Utility of Existing Databases," *Archives of Environmental Health* 47, no. 6 (1992): 398–407; National Research Council, *Science and Judgement in Risk Assessment.*

43. Lois Marie Gibbs, *Love Canal: My Story* (Albany: State University of New York Press, 1982); Adeline Gordon Levine, *Love Canal: Science, Politics, and People* (Lexington, Mass.: Lexington Books, 1982).

44. Beverly Paigen et al., "Prevalence of Health Problems in Children Living Near Love Canal."

45. Beverly Paigen, "Controversy at Love Canal," *Hastings Center Report* 12, no. 3 (1982): 29–37.

46. Wildavsky, *But Is it True?;* Whelan, *Toxic Terror;* Jeffrey R. Smith, "Love Canal Study Attracts Criticism," *Science* 217 (1982): 714–15.

Chapter Three: New Ideas about Nature

1. See David Sachsman, "The Mass Media 'Discover' the Environment: Influences on Environmental Reporting in the First Twenty Years," in *The Symbolic Earth: Discourse and Our Creation of the Environment,* ed. James G. Cantrill and Christine L. Oravec (Lexington: University of Kentucky Press, 1996); Michael R. Edelstein, *Contaminated Communities: The Social and Psychological Impacts of Residential Toxic Exposure* (Boulder, Colo.: Westview Press, 1988).

2. For recollections of people who used to play in the spray, see Sandra Steingraber, *Living Downstream: An Ecologist Looks at Cancer and the Environment* (Reading, Mass.: Addison-Wesley, 1997) 7. For a photo, see John Wargo, *Our Children's Toxic Legacy: How Science and Law Fail to Protect Us from Pesticides* (New Haven, Conn.: Yale University Press, 1996), 41.

3. Allan Mazur, *A Hazardous Inquiry: The Rashomon Effect at Love Canal* (Cambridge, Mass.: Harvard University Press, 1998), 38. As late as 1973, 36.8 percent of respondents to an EPA poll said they would be willing to have a hazardous waste disposal site within one mile of their home, and 27.9 percent were unsure. Only 35 percent were unwilling. See Andrew Szasz, *EcoPopulism: Toxic Waste and the Movement for Environmental Justice* (Minneapolis: University of Minnesota Press, 1994) 14.

4. For reproductions of ads from 1961 about nonrecyclable glass, and a 1949 ad about redwood forests, see Paul Rauber, "New! Improved! Destroys the Environment!" *Sierra* 83, no. 3 (1998): 56–59.

5. Former Senator Gaylord Nelson says that in 1970 he was the only member of Congress with an environmental staff person. By 1995 everyone had one. See the interview with Nelson by Jim Montavalli, "Founding Father: Gaylord Nelson on Earth Day's Past, Present and Future,": *E: The Environmental Magazine* 6, no. 2 (1995): 10ff. On media reporting, see Sachsman, "The Mass Media 'Discover' the Environment."

6. The accident in question occurred at the Fermi plant outside Detroit in 1966. See William Gamson and Andre Modigliani, "Media Discourse and Public Opinion on Nuclear Power: A Constructionist Approach," *American Journal of Sociology* 95 (1989): 1–37.

7. Donald Worster, *Nature's Economy: The Roots of Ecology* (San Francisco: Sierra Club Books, 1977), 40; see also Max Oelschlaeger, *The Idea of Wilderness: From Prehistory to the Age of Ecology* (New Haven, Conn.: Yale University Press, 1991).

8. For a discussion, see the influential essay by Lynn White Jr., "The Historical Roots of Our Ecological Crisis," *Science* 155 (1967): 1203–7.

9. Oelschlaeger, *The Idea of Wilderness*.

10. From Bentham's essay "Principles of the Civil Code," in *The Theory of Legislation* (London: Kegan Paul, Trench, and Trubner 1931), 118.

11. Quoted in Philip Foss, *Politics and Grass: The Administration of Grazing on Public Land* (New York: Greenwood, 1969), 20.

12. Worster, *Nature's Economy*, 202.

13. Anna Bramwell, *Ecology for the 20th Century* (New Haven, Conn.: Yale University Press, 1989); Luc Ferry, *The New Ecological Order* (Chicago: University of Chicago Press, 1995); Roderick Frazier Nash, *Wilderness and the American Mind* (New Haven, Conn.: Yale University Press, 1967).

14. Quoted in Nash, *Wilderness and the American Mind*, pp. 36–37, 37.

15. Quoted in Oelschlaeger, *The Idea of Wilderness*, pp. 185, 186.

16. Eugene Odum's classic book *Fundamentals of Ecology* (Philadelphia: Saunders) first came out in 1953.

17. Samuel P. Hays, *Beauty, Health, and Permanence: Environmental Politics in the United States, 1955–1985* (New York: Cambridge University Press, 1987); Robyn Eckersley, *Environmentalism and Political Theory: Toward an Ecocentric Approach* (Albany: State University of New York Press, 1992); Roderick Frazier Nash, *The Rights of Nature: A History of Environmental Ethics* (Madison: University of Wisconsin Press, 1989); John Dryzek, *The Politics of the Earth: Environmental Discourses* (New York: Oxford University Press, 1997).

18. In the 1930s, they argued that the Dust Bowl was a consequence of ignoring ecology, but they did not warn that the whole earth was in peril. See Worster, *Nature's Economy*, chapter 12.

19. Rachel Carson, *Silent Spring* (Greenwich, Conn.: Fawcett Crest, 1962), 95, 96.

20. Ibid., p. 118–119, 244.

21. Aldo Leopold, *A Sand County Almanac* (New York: Ballantine Books, 1984 [1966]), 238–39, 240.

22. Ibid., pp. 252–253, 259.

23. Barry Commoner, *Science and Survival* (New York: Viking Press, 1967 [1963]), 130.

24. Murray Bookchin, *Our Synthetic Environment* (New York: Knopf, 1974 [1962]), 60.

25. René Dubos, *Man Adapting* (New Haven, Conn.: Yale University Press, 1965), 197, 199.

26. Barry Commoner, *The Closing Circle: Man, Nature, and Technology* (New York: Bantam Books, 1972), 35, 37, 42.

27. Sixty-five people from this range of professions were brought together in San Francisco for a UNESCO conference in November 1969. For their presentations see Huey D. Johnson, ed., *No Deposit, No Return: Man and His Environment: A View Toward Survival* (Reading, Mass.: Addison-Wesley, 1970).

28. By the early seventies, at least ten national environmental organizations had offices in Washington, D.C. Besides those mentioned in the text, the list includes the Natural Resources Defense Council, the Wilderness Society, the Izaak Walton League, the World Wildlife Fund, Friends of the Earth, and the Environmental Policy Center.

29. Robert Gottlieb, *Forcing the Spring: The Transformation of the American Environmental Movement* (Washington, D.C.: Island Press, 1993); Hays, *Beauty, Health and Permanence*.

30. For a lively discussion of the link between environmental ideas and the political visions of the 1960s, see Gottlieb, *Forcing the Spring*, chapter 3.

31. See Steve Chase, "Whither the Radical Ecology Movement?", which serves as the introduction to Murray Bookchin and Dave Foreman, *Defending the Earth: A Dialogue between Murray Bookchin and Dave Foreman* (Boston: South End Press, 1991).

32. For examples of the ecocentrist/deep ecology perspective see Bill Devall and George Sessions, *Deep Ecology: Living As If Nature Mattered* (Salt Lake City: Peregrine Smith Books, 1985); Rik Scarce, *Eco-Warriors: Understanding the Radical Environmental Movement* (Chicago: Noble Press, 1990); George Sessions, ed., *Deep Ecology for the 21st Century* (Boston: Shambhala, 1994); Bill McKibbon, *The End of Nature* (New York: Anchor, 1989); Irene Diamond and Gloria Feman Orenstein, eds., *Reweaving the World: The Emergence of Ecofeminism* (San Francisco: Sierra Club Books, 1990).

33. Arne Naess, "The Place of Joy in a World of Fact," in Sessions, *Deep Ecology for the 21st Century*, p. 250.

34. Devall and Sessions, *Deep Ecology*, p. 7. This view does not overlook political action. Ecocentrism/deep ecology has generated Earth First! the Sea Shepherds, Greenpeace, and the Animal Liberation Front—groups that Rik Scarce calls eco-warriors. Members of these groups express their ecological consciousness in direct action. Their civil disobedience and sabotage pressure governments and industries to adopt environmentalist policies. At the same time, they teach the public that humans are destroying the earth because they do not fully grasp the interdependence of nature. See Scarce, *Eco-Warriors*.

35. See David Pepper, *Eco-Socialism: From Deep Ecology to Social Justice* (London: Routledge, 1993); Bookchin, *Our Synthetic Environment;* Bookchin and Foreman, *Defending the Earth;* Barry Commoner, "The Environment," in *Crossroads: Environmental Priorities for the Future*, ed. Peter Borelli (Washington, D.C.: Island Press, 1998) [originally published in the *New Yorker,* June 15, 1987]; André Gorz, *Ecology As Politics* (Boston: South End Press, 1980); Alain Lipietz, *Green Hopes: The Future of Political Ecology* (Cambridge, England: Polity Press, 1995).

36. Bookchin and Foreman, *Defending the Earth*, p. 128.

37. Bookchin has been writing about eco-anarchy since the early 1960s. For a recent statement of his views see his *Remaking Society: Pathways to a Green Future* (Boston: South End Press, 1990).

38. Commoner, *The Closing Circle*.

39. On the ways that grassroots groups have redefined the environment and enlarged the environmental movement see Giovanna Di Chiro, "Nature As Community: The Convergence of Environmental and Social Justice," in *Uncommon Ground: Toward Reinventing Nature,* ed. William Cronon (New York: W.W. Norton, 1995); Gottlieb, *Forcing the Spring;* Robert D. Bullard, ed., *Unequal Protection: Environmental Justice and Communities of Color* (San Francisco: Sierra Club Books, 1994); Szasz, *EcoPopulism.*

40. Daniel Botkin, *Discordant Harmonies: A New Ecology for the Twenty-First Century* (New York: Oxford University Press, 1990); Michael G. Barbour, "Ecological Fragmentation in the Fifties," in Cronon, *Uncommon Ground.*

41. Cronon, ed., *Uncommon Ground.* p. 51. For other essays in the social constructivist tradition see James G. Cantill and Christine L. Oravec, eds., *The Symbolic Earth: Discourse and Our Creation of the Environment* (Lexington: University Press of Kentucky, 1996); and Barbara Deutsch Lynch, "The Garden and the Sea: U.S. Latino Environmental Discourse and Mainstream Environmentalism," *Social Problems* 40, no. 1 (1993):108–124.

42. Botkin, *Discordant Harmonies,* p. 191.

43. Ibid., p. 26.

44. Bookchin, *Our Synthetic Environment,* pp. 28–29.

45. One place to find the seventeen principles is in an essay by Karl Grossman: "The People of Color Environmental Summit," in Bullard, *Unequal Protection.*

46. Women are marginally more concerned about the environment than are men (but men are more likely to belong to an environmental organization). See Paul Mohai, "Men, Women, and the Environment: An Examination of the Gender Gap in Environmental Concern and Activism," *Society and Natural Resources* 5 (1992): 1–19. Black Americans' concern for the environment is as strong as or stronger than white Americans' (although more whites join environmental organizations). See Robert Emmett Jones and Lewis F. Carter, "Concern for the Environment: An Assessment of Common Assumptions," *Social Science Quarterly* 75 (1994): 560–79.

47. These are the most recent figures as of 1998. The national polls do not ask the same questions every year. For compilations and comments on national polling data about the environment, see Riley E. Dunlap, "Public Opinion in the 1980s: Clear Consensus, Ambiguous Commitments," *Environment* 33, no. 8(1991); Susan Mitchell, *The Official Guide to American Attitudes* (Ithaca, N.Y.: New Strategist Publishing, 1996).

48. See Lester W. Milbrath, *Environmentalists: Vanguard for a New Society* (Albany: State University of New York Press, 1984). These five questions are taken from Appendix C, Table C-1, "Levels of Support for Environmental Values in the U.S. Public in 1980–1982." Milbrath lists twelve questions in the table. Of the seven I do not cover here, two are about the general urgency of environmental problems and five are about support for environmental policies. For those questions, too, the general public agreed with members of environmental organizations.

49. Willett Kempton, James S. Boster, and Jennifer A. Hartley, *Environmental Values in American Culture* (Cambridge, Mass.: MIT Press, 1995), 12. I present selected data from Appendix C in Tables 1–3.

50. Quoted in Dunlap, "Public Opinion in the 1980s," p. 35.

51. Robert Booth Fowler, *The Greening of Protestant Thought* (Chapel Hill: University of North Carolina Press, 1995).

52. C. A. Bowers, *Educating for an Ecologically Sustainable Culture: Rethinking Moral Education, Creativity, Intelligence, and Other Modern Orthodoxies* (Albany: State University of New York Press, 1995).

53. See the EPA's environmental education Web site: http://www.epa.gov/enviroed.

54. David B. Spence, "Paradox Lost: Logic, Morality, and the Foundations of Environmental Law in the 21st Century," *Columbia Journal of Environmental Law* 20, no. 1(1995): 145–81.

55. John Urry, "The Tourist Gaze and the 'Environment,' " *Theory, Culture and Society* 9 (1992): 1–26. One of Urry's points is the irony that ecotourism attracts so many people that it destroys the environment.

56. Donna Lee King, *Doing Their Share to Save the Planet: Children and Environmental Crisis* (New Brunswick, N.J.: Rutgers University Press, 1995).

57. Jennifer Price, "Looking for Nature at the Mall: A Field Guide to the Nature Company," in Cronon, *Uncommon Ground,* p. 188.

58. Robert C. Paehlke, *Environmentalism and the Future of Progressive Politics* (New Haven, Conn.: Yale University Press, 1989).

Chapter Four: Environmentalist Science

1. Thomas Kuhn, *The Structure of Scientific Revolutions* (Chicago: University of Chicago Press, 1970 [1962]). See also Imre Lakatos and Alan Musgrave, eds., *Criticism and the Growth of Knowledge* (Cambridge: Cambridge University Press, 1970); Paul Feyerabend, *Against Method* (London: New Left Books, 1975); Michael M. J. Mulkay, *Science and the Sociology of Knowledge* (London: G. Allen and Unwin, 1979); Sandra Harding, *The Science Question in Feminism* (Ithaca, N.Y.: Cornell University Press, 1986); Bruno Latour, *We Have Never Been Modern* (New York: Harvester Wheatsheaf, 1993); Helen Longino, *Science and Social Knowledge: Values and Objectivity in Social Inquiry* (Princeton, N.J.: Princeton University Press, 1990).

2. Kuhn, *The Structure of Scientific Revolutions,* p. 24.

3. Ibid., p. 111.

4. Ibid., p. 175.

5. See Evelyn Fox Keller, *A Feeling for the Organism: The Life and Work of Barbara Mc-Clintock* (New York: W.H. Freeman, 1983); Evelyn Fox Keller, *Reflections on Gender and Science* (New Haven, Conn.: Yale University Press, 1985), 150–176.

6. Evelyn Fox Keller, "Feminism and Science," in *Sex and Scientific Inquiry,* ed. Sandra Harding and Jean F. O'Barr (Chicago: University of Chicago Press, 1987).

7. Donna Haraway, "Animal Sociology and a Natural Economy of the Body Politic, Part I: A Political Physiology of Dominance," in Harding and O'Barr, *Sex and Scientific Inquiry.* p. 218.

8. Ibid., p. 231.

9. Emily Martin, "The Egg and the Sperm: How Science Has Constructed a Romance Based on Sterotypical Male-Female Roles," *Signs: Journal of Woman in Culture and Society* 16, no. 3 (1991): 485–501. The textbook quotations are on p. 490.

10. Ibid., p. 493.

11. Nancy Krieger and Elizabeth Fee, "Man-Made Medicine and Women's Health: The Biopolitics of Sex/Gender and Race/Ethnicity," *International Journal of Health Services* 24, no. 2 (1994): p. 265–283.

12. Stephen Jay Gould, *The Mismeasure of Man* (New York: W.W. Norton, 1981), 24, 23.

13. Alon Tal, "Assessing the Environmental Movement's Attitudes toward Risk Assessment," *Environmental Science & Technology* 31, no. 10 (1997): 470A–476A. See also Ellen Silbergeld, "The Risks of Risk Assessment," *New Solutions* 3, no. 2 (1993): 43–44, and Theo Colborn, Dianne Dumanoski, and John Peterson Myers, *Our Stolen Future* (New York: Plume/Penguin, 1997).

14. Sander Greenland, ed., *Evolution of Epidemiologic Ideas: Annotated Readings on Concepts and Methods* (Chestnut Hill, Mass.: Epidemiology Resources Inc., 1987); Mervyn Susser and Ezra Susser, "Choosing a Future for Epidemiology: I. Eras and Paradigms," *American Journal of Public Health* 86, no. 5 (1996): 668–673; Mervyn Susser and Ezra Susser, "Choosing a Future for Epidemiology: II. From Black Box to Chinese Boxes and

Eco-Epidemiology," *American Journal of Public Health* 86, no. 5 (1996): 674–677; Sylvia Noble Tesh, *Hidden Arguments: Political Ideology and Disease Prevention Policy* (New Brunswick, N.J.: Rutgers University Press, 1988).

15. Anthony D. Cortese, "Endocrine Disruption," *Environmental Science & Technology* 30, no. 5 (1996): 213A–15A.

16. See Colborn et al., *Our Stolen Future;* and Environmental Protection Agency Office of Research and Development, "Special Report on Environmental Endocrine Disruption: An Effects Assessment and Analysis," EPA/630/R-96/012. Washington, D.C., 1997.

17. Colborn et al., *Our Stolen Future*, p. 247.

18. Ibid., p. 203.

19. Ibid., pp. 169–70.

20. Ibid., p. 203.

21. Ibid., p. 206.

22. Robert R. M. Verchick, "In a Greener Voice: Feminist Theory and Environmental Justice," *Harvard Women's Law Journal* 19 (1996): 23–88.

23. Some people have characterized the focus of research even more narrowly. In an editorial, one of the science editors of *Environmental Health Perspectives* says it has been on "young adult males with an average weight of 70 kg." See Thomas L. Goehl, "Playing in the Sand," *Environmental Health Perspectives* 105 (1997): 564.

24. Natural Resources Defense Council, *Intolerable Risk: Pesticides in Our Children's Food* (Washington, D.C.: NRDC, 1989).

25. National Research Council, *Pesticides in the Diets of Infants and Children* (Washington, D.C.: National Academy Press, 1993).

26. John M. Cushman, "Children's Health Is to Guide EPA," *New York Times*, 12 September 1996, A14.

27. New regulations governing ozone and particulate matter were promulgated on July 16, 1997.

28. Goehl, "Playing in the Sand."

29. U. S. General Accounting Office, *Superfund: Public Health Assessments Incomplete and of Questionable Value*, GAO/RCED-91-178. (Washington, D.C.: GAO, 1991).

30. United Church of Christ/Commission for Racial Justice, *Toxic Wastes and Race in the United States: A National Report on the Racial and Socio-economic Characteristics of Communities with Hazardous Waste Sites* (New York: United Church of Christ/Commission for Racial Justice, 1987).

31. Paul Mohai and Bunyon Bryant, in "Environmental Racism: Reviewing the Evidence," *Race and the Incidence of Environmental Hazards*, ed. Bunyan Bryant and Paul Mohai (Boulder, Colo.: Westview Press, 1992).

32. The best-known critique comes from Vicki Been, "Locally Undesirable Land Uses in Minorty Neighborhoods: Disproportioate Siting or Market Dynamics?" *Yale Law Journal* 102 (April 1994). For reviews of the critiques see Sylvia N. Tesh and Bruce A. Williams, "Identity Politics, Disinterested Politics, and Environmental Justice," *Polity* 18 (1996): 285–305, and Andrew Szasz and Michael Meuser, "Environmental Inequalities: Literature Review and Proposals for New Directions in Research and Theory," *Current Sociology* 45 (1997):99–120.

33. Rebecca Clay Haynes, "The Road to Justice," *Environmental Health Perspectives* 105 (1997): 920–22.

34. See *NAACP-Flint Chapter vs John Engler, governor, State of Michigan,* Circuit Court for the County of Genesee, case number 95-38228-CV; Motion before the Honorable Archie L. Hayman; Flint, Michigan, May 29, 1997.

35. Haynes, "The Road to Justice."

36. Daniel Krewski and Richard D. Thomas, "Carcinogenic Mixtures," *Risk Analysis* 12, no. 1 (1992):105–113; National Research Council, *Science and Judgement in Risk Assessment* (Washington, D.C.: Taylor and Francis, 1996).

37. Maureen C. Hatch, Sylvan Wallenstein, Jan Beyea, Jeri W. Nieves, and Mervyn Susser, "Cancer Rates after the Three Mile Island Nuclear Accident and Proximity of Residence to the Plant," *American Journal of Public Health* 81, no. 6 (1991): 719–24.

38. See Steve Wing, David Richardson, Donna Armstrong, and Douglas Crawford-Brown, "A Re-evaluation of Cancer Incidence Near the Three Mile Island Nuclear Plant: The Collision of Evidence and Assumptions," *Environmental Health Perspectives* 105 (1997): 52–57; Steve Wing, David Richardson, and Donna Armstrong, "A Reply to Comments," *Environmental Health Perspectives* 105 (1997): 266–267.

39. Steven F. Arnold, Diane M. Koltz, Bridgette M. Collins, Peter M. Vonier, Louis J. Guillette Jr., and John A. McLachlan, "Synergistic Activism of Estrogen Receptor with Combinations of Environmental Chemicals," *Science* 272 (1996): 1489–92.

40. Jocelyn Kaiser, "New Yeast Study Finds Strength in Numbers," *Science* 272 (1996) 1489–92.

41. John A. McLachlan, "Synergistic Effect of Environmental Estrogens: Report Withdrawn," *Science* 277 (1997) 1462–63.

42. Gary E. R. Hook and George W. Lucier, "Synergy, Antagonism, and Scientific Process," *Environmental Health Perspectives* 105 (1997): 784.

43. James D. McKinney, "Interactive Hormonal Activity of Chemical Mixes," *Environmental Health Perspecitves* 105(1997): 896.

44. Robert C. Duncan and Barbara S. Hulka, "Biochemical and Biological Markers: Implications for Epidemiologic Studies," *Environmental Health Perspectives* 44, no. 6 (1989): 375–81; Jack D. Griffith, Robert Duncan, and Barbara S. Hulka, *Biological Markers in Epidemiology* (New York: Oxford University Press, 1990); Frederica Perera, "The Potential Usefulness of Biological Markers in Risk Assessment," *Environmental Health Perspectives* 76 (1987): 141–45.

45. National Research Council, "Biological Markers in Environmental Health Research," *Environmental Health Perspectives* 74 (1987): 3.

46. National Research Council, *Environmental Epidemiology: Public Health and Hazardous Waste*, vol. 1 (Washington, D.C.: National Academy Press, 1991), 220–221.

47. Hulka et al, *Biological Markers in Epidemiology;* and Perera, "The Potential Usefulness of Biological Markers in Risk Assessment."

48. In the 1950s the government considered 50 to 60 micrograms of lead per deciliter of blood as normal and 70 to 80 micrograms as dangerous. The numbers moved down as blood-lead studies accumulated. In 1991 the Centers for Disease Control announced that as few as 10 micrograms per deciliter of blood was dangerous. See Barbara Berney, "Round and Round It Goes: The Epidemiology of Childhood Lead Poisoning, 1950–1990," *The Milbank Quarterly* 71, no. 1 (1993): 3–39; David Collingridge and Colin Reeve, *Science Speaks to Power: The Role of Experts in Policy Making* (London: Frances Pinter, 1986).

49. Adeline Gordon Levine, *Love Canal: Science, Politics, and People* (Lexington, Mass.: Lexington Books, 1982); Gina Kolta, "Love Canal: False Alarm Caused by Botched Study," *Science* 208 [1980]:1239–42.

50. Clark W. Heath Jr., Marion R. Nadel, Matthew M. Zack Jr., Andrew T. L. Chen, Michael A. Bender, and R. Julian Preston, "Cytogenic Findings in Persons Living Near Love Canal," *Journal of the American Medical Association* 251 (1984): 1437–40.

51. National Research Council, *Environmental Epidemiology*, p. 224.

52. See National Research Council, *Environmental Epidemiology;* Colin L. Soskoine, "Ethical, Social, and Legal Issues Surrounding Studies of Susceptible Populations and

Individuals," *Environmental Health Perspectives* 105 (1997): 837–41; Harri Vainio and Kirsti Husgafvel-Pursiainen, "Elimination of Environmental Factors or Elimination of Individuals: Biomarkers and Prevention," *Journal of Occupational and Environmental Medicine* 37 (1995): 12–13; Hulka et al., *Biological Markers in Epidemiology;* J. Carl Barrett, "12th Meeting of the Scientific Group on Methodologies for the Safety Evaluation of Chemicals: Susceptibility to Environmental Hazards," *Environmental Health Perspectives* 105, Suppl. 4 (1997): 699–737.

53. Richard A. Cuoto, "Failing Health and New Prescriptions: Community-Based Approaches to Environmental Risks," in *Current Health Policy Issues and Alternatives,* ed. Carol E. Hill (Athens: University of Georgia Press, 1986); David Ozonoff and Leslie I. Boden, "Truth and Consequences: Health Agency Responses to Environmental Health Problems," *Science, Technology, and Human Values* 12, no. 3–4 (1987): 70–77; Carl F. Cranor, "Some Moral Issues in Risk Assessment," *Ethics* 101 (1990): 123–43; David R. Graber and Tim E. Aldrich, "Working with Community Organizations to Evaluate Potential Disease Clusters," *Social Science and Medicine* 37, no. 8 (1993): 1079–85.

54. Cranor, "Some Moral Issues in Risk Assessment."

55. Beverly Paigen, "Controversy at Love Canal," *Hastings Center Report* 12, no. 3 (1982): 32.

56. Peter M. VanDoren, "The Effects of Exposure to 'Synthetic' Chemicals on Human Health: A Review," *Risk Analysis* 16, no. 3 (1996): 367–76.

57. There is of course a third possible relationship between scientific practices and culture. In this one, scientists unconsciously design studies reflective of democratic, egalitarian, environmentalist values. This relation happens—or will happen—when such values are so widely embraced by the general public that they become simple common sense and a science unreflective of them seems, to most people, to have a political agenda.

Chapter Five: Understanding Risk

1. In addition to the enormous problem of simply finding all the groups, there is the problem of deciding what counts as a group. Does it have to have more than one or two members? (A few people with a telephone and some letterhead can have a big impact.) How long does the group need to have been in existence to count? (Suppose it started last Wednesday but even its members think it may fold by next week.) Should we count groups that were once extremely active but now are dormant? (They might spring to life when new developments occur.) What kinds of issues does the group have to be working on to be deemed environmental? (In the early 1990s, no one thought hog farming or urban housing were environmental issues, but now they both are).

2. Being a target of public wrath is a new role for health departments. They enjoyed for as long as anyone can remember a reputation as supporters of public needs. See David Harris, "Health Department: Enemy or Champion of the People?" *American Journal of Public Health* 74, no. 5 (1984): 428–30.

3. Caron Chess, Billie Jo Hance, and Peter M. Sandman, *Improving Dialogue with Communities: A Short Guide for Government Communication* (Trenton: New Jersey Department of Environmental Protection and Energy, 1991); Aaron Wildavsky, *But Is It True? A Citizen's Guide to Environmental Health and Safety Issues* (Cambridge, Mass.: Harvard University Press, 1995).

4. For overviews, see Paul Slovic, "Perception of Risk," *Science* 236 (1987): 280–85; The Royal Society, *Risk: Analysis, Perception and Management* (London: The Royal Society, 1992).

5. See Slovic, "Perception of Risk." See also, Paul Slovic, Baruch Fischhoff, and Sarah Lichtenstein, "Rating the Risks," *Environment* 21, no. 3 (1979): 14–20, 36–39;

Slovic, Fischhoff, and Lichtenstein, "Facts and Fears: Understanding Perceived Risk," in *Societal Assessment: How Safe is Safe Enough?* ed. Richard D. Schwing and Walter A. Albers (New York: Plenum Press, 1980); Slovic, Fischhoff, and Lichtenstein, "Perceived Risk: Psychological Factors and Social Implications," *Proceedings of the Royal Society of London. Series A* (1981): 376.

6. Slovic, "Perception of Risk"; Schwing and Albers, *Societal Assessment;* Vincent T. Covello, "The Perception of Technological Risk: A Literature Review," *Technological Forecasting and Social Change* 23 (1983): 285–97; Charles Perrow, *Normal Accidents: Living with High-Risk Technologies* (New York: Basic Books, 1984); Baruch Fischhoff, "Managing Risk Perceptions," *Issues in Science and Technology II* (1985): 83–96; Environmental Protection Agency, *Unfinished Business: A Comparative Assessment of Environmental Problems* (Washington, D.C., 1987); Brandon B. Johnson and Vincent T. Covello, eds., *The Social and Cultural Construction of Risk* (Dordrecht, The Netherlands: D. Reidel, 1987); Sheldon Krimsky and Dominic Golding, eds., *Social Theories of Risk* (Westport, Conn.: Praeger, 1992).

7. Among the agencies with risk communication guidelines are the U.S. Department of Health and Human Services' Agency for Toxic Substances Disease Registry, (see U.S. Department of Health and Human Services, Agency for Toxic Substances and Disease Registry, *Health Risk Communication Principles and Practices* [Atlanta, Ga., 1994]); New Jersey's Department of Environmental Protection and Energy (see Chess et al., *Improving Dialogue with Communities*); the U.S. Environmental Protection Agency (see Peter M. Sandman, *Explaining Environmental Risk: Some Notes on Environmental Risk Communication* [Washington, D.C.: U.S. EPA Office of Toxic Substances, 1986]); and the (semigovernmental) National Research Council (see National Research Council, *Improving Risk Communication* [Washington, D.C.: National Academy Press, 1989]).

8. Environmental Protection Agency, *Reducing Risk: Setting Priorities and Strategies for Environmental Protection* (Washington, D.C., 1990), 24; June Fessenden-Raden, Janet M. Fitchen, and Jennifer S. Heath, "Providing Risk Information in Communities: Factors Influencing What Is Heard and Accepted," *Science, Technology, and Human Values* 12, no. 3/4 (1987): 94–101; Greg R. Michaud, "Accepting New Technology: Community Relations for Mobile Incineration in Illinois," in *The Analysis, Communication, and Perception of Risk,* ed. B. J. Garrick and Willard C. Gekler (New York: Plenum Press, 1991).

9. James Flynn, Paul Slovic, and C. K. Mertz, "The Nevada Initiative: A Risk Communication Fiasco," *Risk Analysis* 13, no. 5 (1993): 501.

10. K. S. Shrader-Frechette, *Risk and Rationality: Philosophical Foundations for Popular Reforms* (Berkeley: University of California Press, 1991), 78. [Emphasis in original.]

11. Peter M. Sandman, "Informing the Public: Two-Way Environmental Education," *EPA Journal* 17, no. 4 (1991): 39–41. Sandman gives his longest treatment of the distinction between outrage and hazard in *Responding to Community Outrage: Strategies for Effective Risk Communication* (Fairfax, Va.: American Industrial Hygiene Association, 1993).

12. Harry Otway, "Experts, Communication, and Democracy," *Risk Analysis* 7, no. 2 (1987): 125–29; Krimsky and Golding, *Social Theories of Risk;* William Leiss, "Three Phases in the Evolution of Communication Practice," *Annals of the American Academy of the Political and Social Sciences* 545 (1996): 85–94; Baruch Fischhoff, "Perception and Communication Unplugged: Twenty Years of Process," *Risk Analysis* 15, no. 2 (1995): 137–45.

13. Baruch Fischhoff, "Risk: A Guide to Controversy," in National Research Council, *Improving Risk Communication;* Shrader-Frechette, *Risk and Rationality;* Otway, "Experts, Communication, and Democracy"; Brian Wynne, "Public Understanding of Science," in *Handbook of Science and Technology Studies,* ed. Sheila Jasanoff, Gerald E. Markle, James C. Peterson, and Trevor Pinch (New York: Sage Publications, 1992).

14. Paul Slovic, "Public Perception of Risk," *Journal of Environmental Health* 59, no. 9 (1997): 23.

15. Margaret M. Conway, *Political Participation in the U.S.* (Washington, D.C.: Congressional Quarterly Press, 1985); Steven J. Rosenstone and John Mark Hansen, *Mobilization, Participation, and Democracy in America* (New York: Macmillan, 1993).

16. Sidney Verba, "The Voice of the People," *PS: Political Science and Politics* 26, no. 5 (1993): 677–86; Jeffrey M. Berry, *Lobbying for the People: The Political Behavior of Public Interest Groups* (Princeton, N.J.: Princeton University Press, 1977); Frances Fox Piven and Richard Cloward, *Poor People's Movements* (New York: Vintage Press, 1979); Mary Grisez Kweit and Robert W. Kweit, *Implementing Citizen Participation in a Bureaucratic Society* (New York: Praeger, 1981).

17. Lettie M. Wenner, "Environmental Policy in the Courts," in *Environmental Policy in the 1990s*, ed. Norman J. Vig and Michael E. Kraft (Washington, D.C.: Congressional Quarterly Press, 1990); Kay Lehman Schlozman and John Tierney, *Organized Interests and American Democracy* (New York: Harper and Row, 1986), 358–85; Jeffrey M. Berry, *The Interest Group Society* (New York: HarperCollins, 1989), 154–60.

18. Joan B. Aron, "Citizen Participation at Government Expense," *Public Administration Review* 39, no. 5 (1979): 477–85; James Morone, "The Citizen Role in Health Politics," in *Health Politics and Policy*, ed. Theodore J. Litman and Leonard S. Robins (New York: John Wiley, 1984); James L. Creighton, *The Public Involvement Manual* (Cambridge, Mass.: Abt Books, 1981); Marcus E. Ethridge, "Procedures for Citizen Involvement in Environmental Policy: An Assessment of Policy Effects," *Citizen Participation in Public Decision Making*, ed. Jack DeSario and Stuart Langton (New York: Greenwood Press, 1987).

19. Roger W. Cobb and Charles D. Elder, *Participation in American Politics: The Dynamics of Agenda-Building* (Boston: Allyn and Bacon, 1972); Murray Edelman, *The Symbolic Uses of Politics* (Urbana, Ill.: University of Chicago Press, 1976); Deborah Stone, "Causal Stories and the Formation of Policy Agendas," *Political Science Quarterly* 104, no. 2 (1989): 281–300; Sidney Tarrow, *Power in Movement: Social Movements, Collective Action, and Politics* (New York: Cambridge University Press, 1994); Sylvia N. Tesh, "Environmentalism, Pre-environmentalism, and Public Policy," *Policy Sciences* 26 (1993): 1–20.

20. Slovic, Fischhoff, and Lichtenstein, "Rating the Risks."

21. See, for example, Leroy C. Gould, Gerald T. Gardner, Donald R. DeLuca, Adrian R. Tiemann, Leonard W. Doob, and Jan A. J. Stolwijk, *Perceptions of Technological Risks and Benefits* (New York: Russell Sage Foundation, 1988).

22. Rosenstone and Hansen, *Mobilization, Participation, and Democracy in America*, p. 228; Allan J. Cigler and Burdett A. Loomis, "Contemporary Interest Group Politics: More Than 'More of the Same'" in *Interest Group Politics*, 4th ed., ed. Cigler and Loomis (Washington, D.C.: Congressional Quarterly Press, 1995), 394–98; Schlozman and Tierney, *Organized Interests and American Democracy*, pp. 184–97.

23. Many citizen groups do have periodic "lobby days," when hundreds of members gather in Washington or the state capital and swoop down on administrative and legislative offices. Such events deviate from the rule that lobbying is done by staff, but they do exemplify the claim that most citizens participate in policy making through organized groups. At the local level, the generalization that staff do the work is not true because grassroots community groups, almost by definition, have no paid staffs. Thus, the members do the lobbying themselves, but here again, it is groups, not individuals, who lobby.

24. Wenner, "Environmental Policy in the Courts."

25. Morone, "The Citizen Role in Health Politics"; Arthur Brownlea, "Participation: Myths, Realities, and Prognosis," *Social Science and Medicine* 25, no. 6 (1987): 605–14; Peter deLeon, "The Democratization of the Policy Sciences," *Public Administration Review* 52, no. 2 (1992): 125–29.

26. Anne Costain and Steven Majstorovic, "Congress, Social Movements, and Public Opinion: Multiple Origins of Women's Rights Legislation," *Political Research Quarterly* 47 (1994): 111–35; Berry, *The Interest Group Society.*

27. Ron Eyerman and Andrew Jamison, *Social Movements: A Cognitive Approach* (University Park: Pennsylvania State University Press, 1991); Doug McAdam, "The Framing Function of Movement Tactics: Strategic Dramaturgy in the American Civil Rights Movement," in *Comparative Perspectives on Social Movements: Political Opportunities, Mobilizing Structures, and Cultural Framings,* ed. Doug McAdam, John D. McCarthy, and Mayer N. Zald (New York: Cambridge University Press, 1996).

28. Margaret Keck, "Social Equity and Environmental Politics in Brazil," *Comparative Politics* 27, no. 4 (1995): 409–24; Beth A. Conklin and Laura R. Graham, "The Shifting Middle Ground: Amazonian Indians and Eco-Politics," *American Anthropologist* 97, no. 4 (1995): 695–710.

29. David Truman, *Governmental Process, Politics, Interests, and Public Opinion* (New York: Knopf, 1951); John Kingdon, *Agendas, Alternatives, and Public Policies* (Boston: Little, Brown, 1984), 68–71; Rosenstone and Hansen, *Mobilization, Participation, and Democracy in America.*

30. Richard Barke, *Science, Technology, and Public Policy* (Washington, D.C.: Congressional Quarterly Press, 1986); Jack DeSario and Stuart Langton, "Citizen Participation and Technology," in DeSario and Langton, *Citizen Participation in Public Decision Making.*

31. David A. Snow, E. Burke Rochford Jr., Steven K. Worden, and Robert D. Benford, "Frame Alignment Processes, Micromobilization, and Movement Participation," *American Sociological Review* 51 (1986): 464–81; David A. Snow and Robert D. Benford, "Master Frames and 'Cycles of Protest,'" in *Frontiers in Social Movement Theory,* ed. Aldon D. Morris and Carol McClurg Mueller (New Haven, Conn.: Yale University Press, 1992).

32. Michael R. Reich, *Toxic Politics: Responding to Chemical Disasters* (Ithaca, N.Y.: Cornell University Press, 1991); Mayer N. Zald and John D. McCarthy, eds., *The Dynamics of Social Movements* (Cambridge, Mass.: Winthrop, 1979); Edward J. Walsh, Rex Warland, and D. Clayton Smith, "Backyards, NIMBYs, and Incinerator Sitings: Implications for Social Movement Theory," *Social Problems* 40, no. 1 (1993): 25–38.

33. For prominent examples see Wildavsky, *But Is It True?;* Michael Fumento, *Science under Siege: Balancing Technology and the Environment* (New York: William Morrow, 1993); and Edith Efron, *Apocalyptics: Cancer and the Big Lie: How Environmental Politics Controls What We Know about Cancer* (New York: Simon and Schuster, 1984).

34. For details, see the NRDC's quarterly publication, *The Amicus Journal.*

35. The first quote is from a year-end appeal sent in 1987. The second is from a renewal appeal sent in 1988 and signed by George M. Woodwell, director of Woods Hole Oceanographic Institute. As is the custom with such direct mail solicitation, neither letter is dated.

36. Alar is the trade name for daminozide. At issue in the study was its breakdown product, unsymmetrical dimethylhydrazine (UDMH), which the EPA lists as a "probable human carcinogen." Alar was registered as a pesticide, but its purpose was not to deter pests. Instead, it extended the period of time fruits and vegetables remained on the branch, decreased dropping during harvesting, and improved storage life. See Beth Rosenberg, "The Unintended Consequences of Banning Alar," *New Solutions* 6 no. 2 (1996): 34–50.

37. For histories of this event, see Sheila Jasanoff, *The Fifth Branch: Scientific Advisors As Policymakers* (Cambridge, Mass.: Harvard University Press, 1990); Rosenberg, "The Unintended Consequences of Banning Alar"; Kerry E. Rodgers, "Multiple Meanings of Alar after the Scare: Implications for Closure," *Science, Technology, and Human Values* 21, no. 2 (1996): 177–97; Eliot Marshall. "A Is for Apple, Alar, and… Alarmist?" *Science* 254

(1991): 20–22; L. Zeise, P. Painter, P. E. Berteau, A. M. Fan, and R. J. Jackson, "Alar in Fruit: Limited Regulatory Action in the Face of Uncertain Risks," in Garrick and Gekler, *The Analysis, Communication, and Perception of Risk.*

38. Joseph Rosen, "Much Ado about Alar," *Issues in Science and Technology* 7, no. 1 (1990): 85–90.

39. Dr. Frank E. Young, Administrator, U.S. Food and Drug Administration in oral congressional testimony. (See U.S. Senate, Committee on Labor and Human Resources 101st congress "Health Effects of Pesticide Use on Children," Hearing before the Subcommittee on Children, Family, Drugs and Alcoholism, 16 March 1989, p. 23).

40. Dr. John A. Moore, Acting Deputy Administrator, U.S. Environmental Protection Agency, in written congressional testimony. (See U.S. Senate, "Health Effects of Pesticide Use on Children," p. 29.)

41. Charles J. Carey, President of the National Food Processors Association in written congressional testimony. (See U.S. Senate, "Health Effects of Pesticide Use on Children," p. 91.)

42. Marshall, "A Is for Apple, Alar, and... Alarmist?"

43. Natural Resources Defense Council, *Intolerable Risk: Pesticides in Our Children's Food* (Washington, D.C., 1989).

44. Ibid., p. 2.

45. Slovic, Fischhoff, and Lichtenstein, "Rating the Risks," p. 18.

46. Whyatt later left the NRDC to get a doctorate at the Columbia University School of Public Health, and Sewell now has both a master of public health degree and a doctor of law degree from Columbia University.

47. Information on the authors' credentials comes from telephone interviews during December 1994 with Robin Whyatt, Lawrie Mott, Janet Hathaway, John Wargo, and William Nicholson.

48. The peer review committee consisted of Henry Falk, M.D., American Academy of Pediatrics; Joan Gussow, Ed.D., Columbia University; Steven Markowitz, M.D., Mount Sinai School of Medicine; Jack Mayer, M.D., Columbia University; Herbert Needleman, M.D., University of Pittsburgh; Ian Nisbit, Ph.D., Nisbit and Co.; Frederica Perera, Ph.D., Columbia University; Marvin Schneiderman, Ph.D., National Academy of Sciences; Bailus Walker, Ph.D., State University of New York at Albany.

49. U.S. Senate, "Health Effects of Pesticide Use on Children."

50. Zeise et al., "Alar in Fruit."

51. National Research Council, *Pesticides in the Diets of Infants and Children* (Washington, D.C.: National Academy Press, 1993).

52. Nicholas Freudenberg, *Not in Our Backyards!: Community Action for Health and the Environment* (New York: Monthly Review Press, 1984); Gary Cohen and John O'Connor, *Fighting Toxics: A Manual for Protecting Your Family, Community, and Workplace* (Washington, D.C.: Island Press, 1990); Lois Marie Gibbs, *Dying from Dioxin: A Citizen's Guide to Reclaiming Our Health and Rebuilding Democracy* (Boston: South End Press, 1995); Andrew J. Feldman, *The Sierra Club Green Guide* (San Francisco: Sierra Club Books, 1996). Grassroots activists get the same kinds of information from pamphlets and "fact pacts" produced by the Center for Health, Environment and Justice, whose monthly journal regularly lists several dozen of these publications.

53. Nicholas Freudenberg, "Citizen Action for Environmental Health: Report on a Survey of Community Organizations," *American Journal of Public Health* 74, no. 5 (1984): 445.

54. Interview at the Connecticut Citizens Action Group offices in Hartford, Connecticut, November 25, 1987.

55. Telephone interview, June 22, 1992: follow-up on a face-to-face interview the previous year.

56. Interview at the National Wildlife Federation offices in Washington, D.C. March 15, 1988. Jerry Poje is now at the National Institute of Environmental Health Sciences, an agency within the National Institutes of Health.

57. Adeline Gordon Levine, *Love Canal: Science, Politics, and People* (Lexington, Mass.: Lexington Books, 1982).

58. Carol Van Strum, *A Bitter Fog* (San Francisco: Sierra Club, 1983), 95.

59. Phil Brown and Edwin J. Mikkelsen, *No Safe Place: Toxic Waste, Leukemia, and Community Action* (Berkeley: University of California Press, 1990).

60. Reich, *Toxic Politics*.

61. Edward J. Walsh, "Challenging Official Assessments via Protest Mobilization: The TMI Case," in Johnson and Covello, *The Social and Cultural Construction of Risk*.

62. Richard A. Cuoto, "Failing Health and New Prescriptions: Community-Based Approaches to Environmental Risks," in *Current Health Policy Issues and Alternatives* ed. Carol E. Hill (Athens: University of Georgia Press, 1986).

63. Information included in packet presented to the Michigan Department of Environmental Quality by Scio Residents for Safe Water at a public hearing in Ann Arbor, January 13, 1997.

64. Personal communication from the professor in question: Jerome O. Nriagu, Department of Environmental and Industrial Health, University of Michigan School of Public Health.

65. Jeanne Jabanoski, "Citizen Knowledge: Expanding the Base of Data for Environmental Decision-Making" (paper presented at the American Public Health Association annual meeting, Indianapolis, 1997).

Chapter Six: Experiential Knowledge

1. Sylvia N. Tesh and Bruce W. Williams, "Identity Politics, Disinterested Politics, and Environmental Justice," *Polity* 18 (1996): 285–305. Portions of this chapter first appeared in the article.

2. Nancy Leys Stepan and Sander L. Gilman, "Appropriating the Idioms of Science: The Rejection of Scientific Racism," in *The "Racial" Economy of Science: Toward a Democratic Future*, ed. Sandra Harding (Bloomington: Indiana University Press, 1993), 175.

3. Lois N. Magner, "Women and the Scientific Idiom: Textual Episodes from Wollstonecraft, Fuller, Gilman, and Firestone," *Signs: Journal of Women in Culture and Society* 4 (1986): 61–80.

4. On the issue of gatekeepers, see Raymond L. Goldsteen and John K. Schorr, *Demanding Democracy after Three Mile Island* (Gainsville: University of Florida Press, 1991). Goldsteen and Schorr say that after the TMI accident, area residents opposed reopening the facility on the basis that the accident had caused psychological damage. But the psychologists, psychiatrists, and psychiatric epidemiologists who studied the population concluded that no such mental health problems existed. The same thing happened after the PATCO (Professional Air Traffic Controllers Organization) strike in 1981. Air traffic controllers demanded higher pay on the basis that their jobs were stressful. The FAA (Federal Aviation Administration) brought in stress experts to study the situation. The experts determined that the controllers were not under stress. See Chapter 5, "Air Traffic Control and Stress," in Sylvia Noble Tesh, *Hidden Arguments: Political Ideology and Disease Prevention Policy* (New Brunswick, N.J.: Rutgers University Press, 1988).

5. Most of the scholarship on identity politics emphasizes the task of transforming people's self-concept more than the task of transforming policy makers' or the public's ideas. How the replacement occurs is not yet well understood. But, in general, early activists in a social movement help marginalized people create new identities. As people adopt these identities, they come to think of themselves as part of a collectivity. They

then assign political importance to who they are and to what they know about their lives and demand that the general public and policy makers respect that self-definition. These demands mobilize other potential members of the movement, who adopt and promote the new identity, and thereby move the struggle forward. See Craig Calhoun, ed., *Social Theory and the Politics of Identity* (Cambridge, Mass.: Blackwell, 1994), especially the introductory chapter by Calhoun and the chapters by Norbert Wiley and Todd Gitlin. See also Debra Friedman and Doug McAdam, "Collective Identity and Activism: Networks, Choices, and the Life of a Social Movement," in *Frontiers in Social Movement Theory*, ed. Aldon D. Morris and Carol McClurg Mueller (New Haven, Conn.: Yale University Press, 1992); Hank Johnston, Enrique Larana, and Joseph Gusfield, "Identities, Grievances, and New Social Movements," in *New Social Movements: From Ideology to Identity*, ed. Enrique Larana, Hank Johnston, and Joseph R. Gusfield (Philadelphia: Temple University Press, 1994).

6. See the section titled "Consciousness Raising," in *Voices from Women's Liberation*, ed. Leslie B. Tanner (New York: Signet, 1970).

7. The National Welfare Rights Organization (NWRO), which lasted about ten years, collapsed in 1975. Although more welfare recipients are white than black, the NWRO was overwhelmingly black. See Guida West, *The National Welfare Rights Movement: The Social Protest of Poor Women* (New York: Praeger, 1981).

8. Rigoberta Menchu, *I... Rigoberta Menchu: An Indian Woman in Guatemala* (London: Verso, 1984); Domitila Barrios de Chungara, *Let Me Speak: Testimony of Domitila, A Woman of the Bolivian Mines* (New York: Monthly Review Press, 1978). Menchu was later accused of stretching the truth about what she personally experienced (see David Stoll, *Rigoberta Menchu and the Story of All Poor Guatemalans* [Boulder, Colo.: Westview Press, 1999]), but her book still stands as an example of identity politics.

9. "Jerry Lewis, that guy's a real jerk; what they do is portray disability in incredibly negative ways to get people to feel guilty enough to give their money.... But that does irreparable damage to what we are, who we are, and our cause" (quotation from Caroline Wang, "Culture, Meaning and Disability: Injury Prevention Campaigns and the Production of Stigma," *Social Science and Medicine* 35 [1991]: 1096).

10. Also in the late 1970s and early 1980s, some environmentalists began to argue that Native Americans have a special relation to nature, and some feminists began developing a similar argument about women. Neither position redefined environmentalism in the way that grassroots activism did, but each did challenge the initial inclusiveness of the movement. On Native Americans, see Richard Erdoes, *Lame Deer: Seeker of Visions* (New York: Simon and Schuster, 1976); and N. Scott Momaday, "Native American Attitudes toward the Environment," in *Seeing with a Native Eye: Essays on Indian Religion*, ed. Walter Holder Capps (New York: Harper and Row, 1976). On women, see Charlene Spretnak, "Toward an Ecofeminist Spirituality," in *Healing the Wounds: The Promise of Ecofeminism*, ed. Judith Plant (Philadelphia: New Society Publishers, 1989); and Lin Nelson, "The Place of Women in Polluted Places," in *Reweaving the World: The Emergence of Ecofeminism*, ed. Irene Diamond and Gloria Freeman Orenstein (San Francisco: Sierra Club Books, 1990).

11. See Giovanna Di Chiro, "Nature As Community: The Convergence of Environmental and Social Justice," in *Uncommon Ground: Toward Reinventing Nature*, ed. William Cronon (New York: W.W. Norton, 1995); Sandra Steingraber, *Living Downstream: An Ecologist Looks at Cancer and the Environment* (Reading, Mass.: Addison-Wesley, 1997).

12. As I noted in Chapter One, CHEJ was founded in 1980 by Lois Gibbs after she left Love Canal. The organization (called the Citizens Clearinghouse for Hazardous Waste until 1997) offers grassroots groups technical information and training in political organizing.

13. Stephen Lester, "Science Lessons for the Real World," *Everyone's Backyard* 11, no. 4 (1993): 17.

14. Citizens Clearinghouse for Hazardous Waste, *Experts: A User's Guide: Where to Find Them, How to Get Them, How to Pay for Them* (Washington, D.C.: CCHW, 1985), 5. (CCHW is now the Center for Health, Environment and Justice.)

15. Nina Laboy, "Struggle for Survival in the South Bronx," *Everyone's Backyard* 12, no. 2 (1994): 4.

16. Quoted in Cynthia Hamilton, "Concerned Citizens of South Central Los Angeles," in *Unequal Protection: Environmental Justice and Communities of Color,* ed. Robert D. Bullard (San Francisco, Sierra Club Books, 1994), 209. [Ellipses in the original.]

17. Quoted in Celine Kraus, "Women of Color on the Front Line," in Bullard, *Unequal Protection,* p. 261.

18. The community in question was Yellow Creek, Kentucky. The quotation is in Phil Brown and Edwin J. Mikkelsen, *No Safe Place: Toxic Waste, Leukemia, and Community Action* (Berkeley: University of California Press, 1990), 129.

19. "Too Little, Too Late," *Everybody's Backyard* 15, no. 1 (1997): 16. [Ellipses in original.]

20. Quoted in Brown and Mikkelsen, *No Safe Place,* p. 145.

21. Quoted in Rick Bragg, "Pollution Drives Away Neighborhood and Trust," *New York Times,* 16 March 1997, A16.

22. Interview with Kathy Milberg, Executive Director of Southwest Detroit Environmental Vision, on October 20, 1997.

23. The Albuquerque meeting was called by the Southwest Organizing Project in the fall of 1986. The quotation is from Michael Guerrero and Louis Head, "Organizing the Frontlines," in *We Speak for Ourselves: Social Justice, Race, and Environment,* ed. Dana Alston (Washington, D.C.: The Panos Institute, 1990), 34.

24. Hamilton, "Concerned Citizens of South Central Los Angeles," p. 215.

25. Symposium on Health Research Needs to Ensure Environmental Justice, February 10–12, 1994. The symposium was sponsored by the National Institute of Environmental Health Sciences, the NIH Office of Minority Health Research, the Environmental Protection Agency, the National Institute for Occupational Safety and Health, the Agency for Toxic Substances and Disease Registry, the U.S. Department of Energy, and the National Center for Environmental Health. The coleaders were Bunyon Bryant from the University of Michigan and Jerry Poje from the National Institute of Environmental Health Sciences. Symposium proceedings are available from the National Institute of Environmental Health Sciences, P.O. Box 12233, Research Triangle Park, NC 27709. I attended the symposium, and my account of the events comes from the published proceedings, from my own notes, and from an interview with Bunyon Bryant in August 1998.

26. See Bullard, *Unequal Protection;* Bunyan Bryant and Paul Mohai, eds., *Race and the Incidence of Environmental Hazards* (Boulder, Colo.: Westview Press, 1992).

27. Proceedings of the Symposium on Health Research Needs to Ensure Environmental Justice, pp. 11, 12, 13 (see note 25, above).

28. See page 41 of the symposium proceedings. The quotation here may not be his exact words. The published conference proceedings are mainly paraphrases of the speakers' comments. In most cases, it is impossible to tell which words were actually spoken.

29. Symposium proceedings, p. 9. As noted above, these may not be Dr. Murray's exact words.

30. Ken Sexton, director of the EPA office of health research. See the symposium proceedings, p. 6. Here again, these may not have been his exact words.

31. Symposium proceedings, pp. 16, 22.

32. Studs Turkel, *Race: How Blacks and Whites Think and Feel about the American Obsession* (New York: Anchor Books, 1991), p. 5.

33. On the Ryan White case and others in which parents and city officials worked to prevent HIV-positive children from attending school, see Dianne L. Kerr, "Ryan White's Death: A Time to Reflect on School's [*sic*] Progress in Dealing with AIDS," *Journal of School Health* 60 (1990): 237–238.

34. Martha R. Fowlkes and Patricia Y. Miller, "Chemicals and Community at Love Canal," in *The Social and Cultural Construction of Risk*, ed. Brandon B. Johnson and Vincent T. Covello (Dordrecht, The Netherlands: D. Reidel, 1987), p. 73. As for having different experiential knowledge, one Love Canal resident told Fowlkes and Miller, "I had the surgery done in the winter and then, after I got done with my treatments, I wound up with infections and other problems.... It's possible it could be related to the chemicals. I never gave it much thought, 'cause really what happened to us could happen anywhere in the country, right?" (p. 67).

35. For an organizer's perspective on this issue, see Lee Staples, *Roots to Power: A Manual for Grassroots Organizing* (New York: Praeger, 1984). For a theorist's perspective, see John D. McCarthy and Mayer N. Zald, "Resource Mobilization and Social Movements: A Partial Theory," *American Journal of Sociology* 82, no. 6 (1977):1212–41; and Edward Walsh, "Resource Mobilization and Citizen Protest around Three Mile Island," *Social Problems* 29 (1991): 1–21.

36. Citizens Clearinghouse for Hazardous Waste, *Experts*, p. 2.

37. Karl Marx, "The German Ideology: Part I," in *The Marx-Engels Reader*, ed. Robert C. Tucker (New York: W.W. Norton, 1978), 172. (Later scholars, most famously Antonio Gramsci and Michel Foucault, came to similar conclusions.)

38. Raymond Williams, "Selections from *Marxism and Literature*," in *Culture/Power/History: A Reader in Contemporary Social Theory*, ed. Nicholas B. Dirks, Geoff Eley, and Sherry B. Ortner (Princeton, N.J.: Princeton University Press, 1994).

39. Nancy C. M. Hartsock, *Money, Sex, and Power: Toward a Feminist Historical Materialism* (Boston: Northeastern University Press, 1983), 234.

40. Nancy C. M. Hartsock, "The Feminist Standpoint: Developing the Ground for a Specifically Feminist Historical Materialism," in *Discovering Reality: Feminist Perspectives on Epistemology, Metaphysics, Methodology, and Philosophy of Science*, ed. Sandra Harding and Merrill B. Hintikka (Dordrecht, The Netherlands: D. Reidel, 1983).

41. Sandra Harding, *Whose Science? Whose Knowledge? Thinking from Women's Lives* (Ithaca, N.Y.: Cornell University Press, 1991). Hartsock and Harding both recognize the class, racial, sexual-orientation, and national divisions among women, but, along with other feminist scholars, they argue that the resulting multiplicity of feminist standpoints can strengthen women's struggle to overcome patriarchy. For feminist scholars making similar arguments about women's unique view of the world, see Emily Martin, *The Woman in the Body: A Cultural Analysis of Reproduction* (Boston: Beacon Press, 1987); and Allison M. Jaeger, *Feminist Politics and Human Nature* (Sussex, England: Harvester Press, 1983).

42. To be sure, some feminists and some gays and lesbians have used essentialist arguments as a political tactic to gain equal rights, but the strategy is highly controversial. See Calhoun, *Social Theory and the Politics of Identity*, pp. 12–20.

43. Possibly, of course, the record is just missing. Perhaps many people at mid-century had intuitive knowledge about the health effects of pollution but more-powerful social actors successfully kept the issue off the political agenda. Peter Bachrach and Morton Baratz wrote an influential article describing that kind of political power (Bachrach and Baratz, "Two Faces of Power," *American Political Science Review* 56 [1962]: 947–952). And Steven Lukes elaborated their point (Steven Lukes, *Power: A Radical View* [London:

Macmillan, 1974]). Since those works were published policy analysts have become cautious about labeling something a nonissue. But in the case of the health effects of environmental pollution, it is a good guess that no one had to work to suppress the issue forty years ago. As Michael R. Reich has shown, when something once kept off the agenda finally becomes a public issue, the people who were alert to the situation beforehand come forward and say so (Reich, *Toxic Politics: Responding to Chemical Disasters* [Ithaca, N.Y.: Cornell University Press, 1991]). This coming forward has not happened for environmental health issues. People are not saying they knew all along, or their parents knew all along, that synthetic chemicals pose a serious health hazard. They say, aghast, "Can you believe we played in the fog behind those DDT trucks?"

44. Di Chiro, "Nature As Community"; Robert Gottlieb, *Forcing the Spring: The Transformation of the American Environmental Movement* (Washington, D.C.: Island Press, 1993); Michael E. Edelstein, *Contaminated Communities: The Social and Psychological Impacts of Residential Toxic Exposure* (Boulder, Colo.: Westview Press, 1988).

45. Tesh, *Hidden Arguments,* chapters 1, 2; Nancy Tomes, *The Gospel of Germs: Men, Women, and the Microbe in American Life* (Cambridge, Mass.: Harvard University Press, 1998).

Chapter Seven: Social Movements and Social Change

1. Hadley Cantril, *The Psychology of Social Movements* (New York: J. Wiley and Sons, 1941); Neil Smelser, *Theory of Collective Behavior* (New York: Free Press, 1962); Ted R. Gurr, *Why Men Rebel* (Princeton, N.J.: Princeton University Press, 1970).

2. The term *meddlesome fanatics* comes from a book that tried to rescue abolitionists from their previous reputation among historians; see Martin Duberman, ed., *The Antislavery Vanguard: New Essays on the Abolitionists* (Princeton, N.J.: Princeton University Press, 1965), vii. For an example of the earlier, derogatory literature see Avery O. Craven, *Civil War in the Making, 1815–1860* (Baton Rouge: Louisiana State University Press, 1959).

3. For some of the classic resource mobilization literature see John D. McCarthy and Mayer N. Zald, "Resource Mobilization and Social Movements: A Partial Theory," *American Journal of Sociology* 82 (1977); Charles Tilly, *From Mobilization to Revolution* (Reading, Mass.: Addison-Wesley, 1978); Anthony Overschall, *Social Conflict and Social Movements* (Englewood Cliffs, N.J.: Prentice-Hall, 1973); William Gamson, *The Strategy of Social Protest* (Homewood, Ill.: Dorsey, 1975). For a specific application to the grassroots toxics movement see Edward J. Walsh, Rex Warland, and D. Clayton Smith, "Backyards, NIMBYs and Incinerator Sitings: Implications for Social Movement Theory," *Social Problems* 40, no. 1 (1993): 25–38.

4. For an overview of the political opportunity literature see Doug McAdam, "Conceptual Origins, Current Problems, Future Directions," in *Comparative Perspectives on Social Movements: Political Opportunities, Mobilizing Structures, and Cultural Framings* ed. Doug McAdam, John D. McCarthy, and Mayer N. Zald (New York: Cambridge University Press, 1996).

5. Herbert P. Kitchelt, "Political Opportunity Structures and Political Protest: Anti-Nuclear Movements in Four Democracies," *British Journal of Political Science* 16 (1986):57–85; Charles Tilly, "Social Movements and National Politics," in *Statemaking and Social Movements,* ed. Charles Bright and Susan Harding (Ann Arbor: University of Michigan Press, 1984).

6. Alain Touraine, *The Voice and the Eye: An Analysis of Social Movements* (Cambridge: Cambridge University Press, 1981); Alberto Melucci, *Nomads of the Present: Social Movements and Individual Needs in Contemporary Society* (Philadelphia: Temple University Press, 1989); Jean L. Cohen, "Strategy or Identity: New Theoretical Paradigms and

Contemporary Social Movements," *Social Research* 52 (1985):663–716. For an excellent collection of articles examining social movements from a social constructivist perspective, see Aldon D. Morris and Carol McClurg Mueller, eds., *Frontiers in Social Movement Theory* (New Haven, Conn.: Yale University Press, 1992).

7. Erving Goffman, *Frame Analysis: An Essay on the Organization of Experience* (New York: Harper Colophon, 1974), 21, 10.

8. William A. Gamson, *Talking Politics* (Cambridge: Cambridge University Press, 1992); Frances Fox Piven and Richard Cloward, *Poor People's Movements* (New York: Vintage Press, 1979); Sidney Tarrow, *Power in Movement: Social Movements, Collective Action, and Politics* (Cambridge: Cambridge University Press, 1994).

9. David A. Snow, E. Burke Rochford Jr., Steven K. Worden, and Robert D. Benford, "Frame Alignment Processes, Micromobilization, and Movement Participation," *American Sociological Review* 51 (1986):464–81.

10. Tarrow, *Power in Movement.*

11. Stella Čapek, "The 'Environmental Justice' Frame: A Conceptual Discussion and an Application," *Social Problems* 40, no. 1 (1993): 2–24.

12. Sheila Foster, "Justice from the Ground Up: Distributive Justice Inequities, Grassroots Resistance, and the Transformative Politics of the Environmental Justice Movement," *California Law Review* 86 (1998):776–841. Unlike Čapek, Foster criticizes the environmental justice frame. She says it masks the mechanisms and processes that result in unequal exposures to environmental pollution.

13. Sam Marullo, Ron Pagnucco, and Jackie Smith, "Frame Changes and Social Movement Contraction: U.S. Peace Movement Framing after the Cold War," *Sociological Inquiry* 66, no. 1 (1996):1–28. See also Mario Diani, "Linking Mobilization Frames and Political Opportunities: Insights from Regional Populism in Italy," *American Sociological Review* 61 (1996):1053–69.

14. On the peace movement, see James Turner Johnson, *The Quest for Peace: Three Moral Traditions in Western Cultural History* (Princeton, N.J.: Princeton University Press, 1987); Gerardo Zampaglioni, *The Idea of Peace in Antiquity* (Notre Dame: University of Indiana Press, 1973); C. Roland Marchand, *The American Peace Movement and Social Reform, 1898–1918* (Princeton, N.J.: Princeton University Press, 1972). On the equality movement, see Ernest G. Bormann, *Forerunners of Black Power: The Rhetoric of Abolition* (Englewood Cliffs, N.J., Prentice-Hall, 1971); Celeste Michelle Condit and John Lewis Lucaites, *Crafting Equality: America's Anglo-African Word* (Chicago: University of Chicago Press, 1993); Gerda Lerner, *The Grimke Sisters from South Carolina: Rebels against Slavery* (Boston: Houghton Mifflin, 1967).

15. For example, see Ron Eyerman and Andrew Jamison, *Social Movements: A Cognitive Approach* (University Park: Pennsylvania State University Press, 1991); Thomas R. Rochon, *Culture Moves: Ideas, Activism, and Changing Values* (Princeton, N.J.: Princeton University Press, 1998).

16. Charles Tilly, *European Revolutions 1492–1992* (Oxford: Blackwell, 1993).

17. David A. Snow and Robert D. Benford, "Master Frames and 'Cycles of Protest,'" in Morris and Mueller, *Frontiers in Social Movement Theory,* p. 136.

18. Karl-Werner Brand, "Cyclical Aspects of New Social Movements: Waves of Cultural Criticism and Mobilization Cycles of New Middle-Class Activism," in *Challenging the Political Order: New Social and Political Movements in Western Democracies,* ed. Russell J. Dalton and Manfred Keuchler (New York: Oxford University Press, 1990), 39.

19. Ronald Inglehart, "Values, Ideology, and Cognitive Mobilization in New Social Movements," in Dalton and Keuchler, *Challenging the Political Order,* p. 45.

20. Stephen Cotgrove and Andrew Duff, "Environmentalism, Middle-Class Radicalism, and Politics," *Sociological Review* 28 (1980): 339.

21. Steven Lukes, *Power: A Radical View* (London: Macmillan, 1974), 23.

22. Antonio Gramsci, *Selections from the Prison Notebooks* (New York: International Publishers, 1971), 157, 327.

23. Michel Foucault, *Power/Knowledge*, reprinted as "Lecture Two" in Nicholas B. Dirks, Geoff Eley, and Sherry B. Ortner, eds., *Culture/Power/History: A Reader in Contemporary Social Theory* (Princeton, N.J.: Princeton University Press, 1994), 210–11, quotation p. 211.

24. Pierre Bourdieu, *Outline of a Theory of Practice*, trans. Richard Nice (Cambridge: Cambridge University Press, 1977), 164. Foucault, "Lecture Two."

25. Carl Boggs, *Social Movements and Political Power: Emerging Forms of Radicalism in the West* (Philadelphia: Temple University Press, 1986), 5.

26. Ibid., pp. 47–57.

27. Rochon, *Culture Moves*, pp. xv, 24–25.

28. Ibid., pp. 30–31.

29. Eyerman and Jamison, *Social Movements*, p. 4.

30. Ibid., pp. 55, 100–101.

31. Ibid., pp. 104–6.

32. William A. Gamson, *The Strategy of Social Protest* (Belmont, Calif.: Wadsworth, 1989); Todd Gitlin, *The Whole World Is Watching: The Media in the Making and Unmaking of the New Left* (Berkeley: University of California Press, 1980).

33. Michael H. Brown, *Laying Waste: The Poisoning of America by Toxic Chemicals* (New York: Pantheon Books, 1980).

34. Rochon, *Culture Moves*.

Index